Human Development

YOUR BODY How It Works

YOUR BODY
How It Works

Human Development

Ted Zerucha, Ph.D.

Introduction by
Denton A. Cooley, M.D.
President and Surgeon-in-Chief
of the Texas Heart Institute
Clinical Professor of Surgery at the
University of Texas Medical School, Houston, Texas

CHELSEA HOUSE
P U B L I S H E R S
A Haights Cross Communications Company
Philadelphia

CHELSEA HOUSE PUBLISHERS
VP, NEW PRODUCT DEVELOPMENT Sally Cheney
DIRECTOR OF PRODUCTION Kim Shinners
CREATIVE MANAGER Takeshi Takahashi
MANUFACTURING MANAGER Diann Grasse

Staff for HUMAN DEVELOPMENT
EDITOR Beth Reger
PRODUCTION EDITOR Megan Emery
PHOTO EDITOR Sarah Bloom
SERIES & COVER DESIGNER Terry Mallon
LAYOUT 21st Century Publishing and Communications, Inc.

www.chelseahouse.com

First Printing

1 3 5 7 9 8 6 4 2

Library of Congress Cataloging-in-Publication Data

Zerucha, Ted, 1967–
    Human development/by Ted Zerucha.
       p. cm. — (Your body, how it works)
Includes bibliographical references and index.
Contents: The delicate embryo—What is development?—The starting
point of development: the cell—The first steps to multicellularity—
The most important time of your life?—The beginnings of the central
nervous system—Establishing the axes—Limb development.
    ISBN 0-7910-7631-8
    1. Embryology, Human—Juvenile literature. [1. Embryology, Human.
2. Fetus.] I. Title. II. Series.
QM601.Z47 2003
612.6'4—dc22
                                                    2003016579

Table of Contents

Introduction

The human body is an incredibly complex and amazing structure. At best, it is a source of strength, beauty, and wonder. We can compare the healthy body to a well-designed machine whose parts work smoothly together. We can also compare it to a symphony orchestra in which each instrument has a different part to play. When all of the musicians play together, they produce beautiful music.

From a purely physical standpoint, our bodies are made mainly of water. We are also made of many minerals, including calcium, phosphorous, potassium, sulfur, sodium, chlorine, magnesium, and iron. In order of size, the elements of the body are organized into cells, tissues, and organs. Related organs are combined into systems, including the musculoskeletal, cardio-vascular, nervous, respiratory, gastrointestinal, endocrine, and reproductive systems.

Our cells and tissues are constantly wearing out and being replaced without our even knowing it. In fact, much of the time, we take the body for granted. When it is working properly, we tend to ignore it. Although the heart beats about 100,000 times per day and we breathe more than 10 million times per year, we do not normally think about these things. When something goes wrong, however, our bodies tell us through pain and other symptoms. In fact, pain is a very effective alarm system that lets us know the body needs attention. If the pain does not go away, we may need to see a doctor. Even without medical help, the body has an amazing ability to heal itself. If we cut ourselves, the blood clotting system works to seal the cut right away, and the immune defense system sends out special blood cells that are programmed to heal the area.

During the past 50 years, doctors have gained the ability to repair or replace almost every part of the body. In my own field of cardiovascular surgery, we are able to open the heart and repair its valves, arteries, chambers, and connections. In many cases, these repairs can be done through a tiny "keyhole" incision that speeds up patient recovery and leaves hardly any scar. If the entire heart is diseased, we can replace it altogether, either with a donor heart or with a mechanical device. In the future, the use of mechanical hearts will probably be common in patients who would otherwise die of heart disease.

Until the mid-twentieth century, infections and contagious diseases related to viruses and bacteria were the most common causes of death. Even a simple scratch could become infected and lead to death from "blood poisoning." After penicillin and other antibiotics became available in the 1930s and 40s, doctors were able to treat blood poisoning, tuberculosis, pneumonia, and many other bacterial diseases. Also, the introduction of modern vaccines allowed us to prevent childhood illnesses, smallpox, polio, flu, and other contagions that used to kill or cripple thousands.

Today, plagues such as the "Spanish flu" epidemic of 1918–19, which killed 20 to 40 million people worldwide, are unknown except in history books. Now that these diseases can be avoided, people are living long enough to have long-term (chronic) conditions such as cancer, heart failure, diabetes, and arthritis. Because chronic diseases tend to involve many organ systems or even the whole body, they cannot always be cured with surgery. These days, researchers are doing a lot of work at the cellular level, trying to find the underlying causes of chronic illnesses. Scientists recently finished mapping the human genome, which is a set of coded "instructions" programmed into our cells. Each cell contains 3 billion "letters" of this code. By showing how the body is made, the human genome will help researchers prevent and treat disease at its source, within the cells themselves.

The body's long-term health depends on many factors, called risk factors. Some risk factors, including our age, sex, and family history of certain diseases, are beyond our control. Other important risk factors include our lifestyle, behavior, and environment. Our modern lifestyle offers many advantages but is not always good for our bodies. In western Europe and the United States, we tend to be stressed, overweight, and out of shape. Many of us have unhealthy habits such as smoking cigarettes, abusing alcohol, or using drugs. Our air, water, and food often contain hazardous chemicals and industrial waste products. Fortunately, we can do something about most of these risk factors. At any age, the most important things we can do for our bodies are to eat right, exercise regularly, get enough sleep, and refuse to smoke, overuse alcohol, or use addictive drugs. We can also help clean up our environment. These simple steps will lower our chances of getting cancer, heart disease, or other serious disorders.

These days, thanks to the Internet and other forms of media coverage, people are more aware of health-related matters. The average person knows more about the human body than ever before. Patients want to understand their medical conditions and treatment options. They want to play a more active role, along with their doctors, in making medical decisions and in taking care of their own health.

I encourage you to learn as much as you can about your body and to treat your body well. These things may not seem too important to you now, while you are young, but the habits and behaviors that you practice today will affect your physical well-being for the rest of your life. The present book series, YOUR BODY: HOW IT WORKS, is an excellent introduction to human biology and anatomy. I hope that it will awaken within you a lifelong interest in these subjects.

Denton A. Cooley, M.D.
President and Surgeon-in-Chief
of the Texas Heart Institute
Clinical Professor of Surgery at the
University of Texas Medical School, Houston, Texas

1

The Delicate Embryo

Development is the process by which a single cell becomes a multicellular organism. In humans, this process takes approximately 264 days, or 9 months. During that time, a single cell divides many times to produce many cells. These cells undergo a limitless number of events at the cellular, molecular, and genetic levels to shape this collection of cells into the form of a human. Development begins with **fertilization**, the fusion of a sperm cell with an egg cell. Fertilization produces the first cell that, in turn, will ultimately give rise to every cell in the body. This first cell and its **progeny** will go on to make important decisions at the molecular level as they divide and take on specific fates. Some cells will take on a neural fate, some cells will become muscle, and some cells will become skin. This collection of cells, the embryo, will take on form, and cells will begin to position themselves to reflect the eventual role they will take as development proceeds. Cells destined to become muscle will position themselves inside the embryo while cells destined to become skin will position themselves on the outside of the embryo. Axes will form that will define the front and back, left and right, and top and bottom of the developing embryo. The nervous system will form as will organs, and throughout this entire process the embryo and then fetus will continue to grow.

Human development can be divided into three distinct phases or stages: the **pre-embryonic stage**, the **embryonic stage**, and the fetal stage. The first two weeks of development are known as the pre-embryonic stage and precede the implantation of the embryo into the uterus of the mother following fertilization. The time from the beginning of week three to the end of week eight is known as the embryonic stage. It is during this time that the embryo undergoes many developmental events that transform a mass of cells into human form. From the end of the eighth week until birth, the developing human is called a **fetus**. This time span largely consists of growth as the inch long but distinctly human-appearing fetus with its well-formed face, limbs, hands, and feet develops and matures in preparation for birth.

The degree of progress made within the field of developmental biology in recent years has been remarkable. Advances in cell and molecular biology have provided insights into the mechanisms that control physical, developmental events that previously could only been observed in wonder. Simply observing the development of a living **embryo** is an awe-inspiring experience when merely the outward physical form is considered. The recognition that a limitless number of events at the cellular, molecular, and genetic levels are controlling the development of this form brings with it a realization that there is a hidden complexity underlying what is being observed. Development involves a complex array of pathways and processes that interact together in the correct place and with the correct timing to produce the mechanisms that construct the embryo.

To fully understand the process of development, it is also necessary to understand the delicacy of the embryo. The developmental process by which a single cell becomes an embryo and ultimately an adult is delicate and finely balanced. Evidence to support this comes in many forms, the most obvious being how easily development can be disrupted. It is estimated that approximately 2% of human infants are born with some kind of observable physical abnormality. Examples of some of these abnormalities include missing limbs, missing or additional fingers and/or

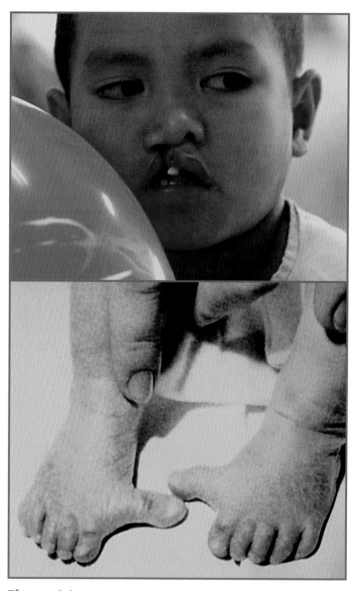

Figure 1.1 These photos illustrate some examples of human birth defects. In the top photograph, a young boy has a cleft lip, characterized by the opening in the upper lip between the mouth and nose. The bottom photo shows a child with polydactyly, (the presence of extra fingers or toes). In this case the child was born with six toes on each foot instead of five.

toes, cleft palate, cleft lip, and spina bifida (Figure 1.1). In addition, it is estimated that greater than 50% of pregnancies result in a miscarriage.

These abnormalities and miscarriages are caused by several factors. The genetic makeup of the developing embryo affects many of the developmental processes. Just as the developing embryo inherits the instructions for its future hair and eye color from its parents, it is also possible for the embryo to inherit information that has been changed or mutated, which can potentially lead to some kind of abnormality or even to its termination.

The conditions, or environment, in which the embryo develops also play a role in its development. During the past several decades, the public has become aware that substances taken in by a pregnant woman can potentially have serious consequences on the developing embryo. For example, pregnant women are advised not to smoke or drink alcohol so as not to harm the child they carry. Many over-the-counter and prescription medications are also potentially harmful to a developing human, and many medications carry warning labels that they should not be used by pregnant women for this very reason.

One example of the serious consequences that outside agents can potentially have on human development occurred in the 1950s when a drug company in Germany developed a drug called thalidomide. Because scientists working for this company found that they could treat laboratory animals with extremely high doses of thalidomide with virtually no effect on the animal, thalidomide was declared to be non-toxic and therefore safe. Thalidomide was prescribed to pregnant women suffering from morning sickness, nervousness, or insomnia. In fact, the company that developed thalidomide, as well as its distributors, declared it to be the best and safest drug for pregnant women.

Within a year of thalidomide becoming available to the

general public, medical doctors began noticing an increase in the number of babies born with **phocomelia**, which was considered to be a rare birth defect. Phocomelia is characterized by the hands and feet of the child being attached to abbreviated, or shortened, arms and legs (Figure 1.2). In extreme cases, the limbs may be completely absent with the hands and feet attached directly to the trunk of the body. This physical appearance associated with phocomelia is the basis for its name that combines *phoco-* (Greek "seal") and *melia* (Greek "limb") to describe the deformed limb's

A DRUG IN SEARCH OF A DISEASE

During the early to mid-1950s, a drug company in Germany developed the drug called thalidomide. This drug was interesting as scientists working for this company found that they could treat laboratory animals with extremely high doses of thalidomide with virtually no effect on the animal. Because of this, thalidomide was declared to be non-toxic and therefore very safe. The problem, of course, was that a drug that did not do anything would be of little use for anything! Despite this, the non-toxicity of thalidomide was attractive enough to encourage the company scientists to try to find a use for it, and thalidomide essentially became a cure in search of a disease. One use that it was tested for was as an anticonvulsant for epileptics. Patients who suffered from epilepsy were given thalidomide and, while it did not prevent their convulsions, it did cause them to go into a deep sleep. This observation was very exciting as the 1950s also saw the advent of the development of tranquilizers and sleeping pills. A very large percentage of the population, particularly in North America and Europe, were regularly using these medications. Tranquilizers and sleeping pills had a dark side, however. The majority of tranquilizers were barbiturates, which are not only addictive but can be lethal when taken at a dosage not much greater than the normal dose. Because of this, the increase in people using these similar appearance to the flippers of a seal. Phocomelia is an extremely rare birth defect, estimated to occur once in approximately four million births. In fact, the incidence of phocomelia is so low that it is likely that most physicians would never even observe a case of it during their entire careers. Thus it was with great surprise that physicians might see a number of such cases or become aware of several such births occurring within a certain region in a very short time span. To determine the cause behind this epidemic of phocomelia, comparisons were made in an

drugs was also accompanied by an increase in deaths associated with the accidental as well as deliberate overdosing of these pharmaceutical agents.

This toxic side effect of barbiturates was, naturally, a very large concern to pharmaceutical companies. Thus the discovery that the non-toxic thalidomide acted similarly to these drugs, but without the negative side effects, was met with a great deal of excitement. Very quickly this drug was released onto the market where, alone or in combination with other drugs, it was sold and utilized as a completely safe remedy for ailments such as the flu, colds, headaches, anxiety, and of course sleeplessness. Thalidomide was marketed under a number of different brand names that eventually expanded into international markets, ultimately becoming available in close to fifty countries throughout Europe, Asia, Africa, and the Americas. Its biggest selling point was its complete safety; it was considered to be impossible to take a toxic dose. Because of this apparent safety, thalidomide eventually started being prescribed to pregnant women suffering from morning sickness, nervousness, or insomnia. In fact, the company that developed thalidomide, as well as its distributors, declared it to be the best and safest drug for pregnant women.

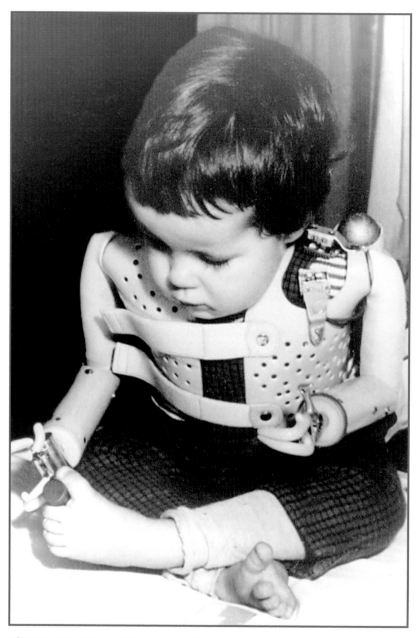

Figure 1.2 This child was born with birth defects resulting from the use of the teratogen thalidomide by the mother during the pregnancy. Due to the drug's effects of development, the child is lacking hands and arms.

attempt to discover some common element shared by the mothers who carried and gave birth to these deformed infants. The one common element to these births was that the mothers all used a medication that contained thalidomide during their pregnancy.

Thalidomide was available to the general public for approximately four years (1957–1961). It is estimated that during the time thalidomide was being used, at least 8,000–12,000 babies were born with birth defects as a direct result of their mothers using medications that contained thalidomide. Less than half of these children survived past their childhood. These statistics do not take into account the number of children born with internal damage caused by thalidomide, nor do they take into account the number of pregnancies that did not come to term as a result of the damage to the embryo caused by the drug. Conservative estimates, taking these additional factors into consideration, triple the number of pregnancies affected by thalidomide.

The story of thalidomide is heartbreaking and tragic, but clearly illustrates that a woman must exercise caution during pregnancy. Thalidomide was considered to be very safe and yet it had a very unexpected and horrible underside. Cautions against other agents such as alcohol, cigarettes, and certain medications that are also known to cause birth defects should be taken very seriously. Embryonic development is incredibly sensitive. Outside agents, such as thalidomide, can alter normal developmental events even at very low doses (one dose of thalidomide taken once during pregnancy was enough to cause birth defects). Agents that can disrupt development and lead to birth defects are called **teratogens** (Greek word for "monster formers"). These agents can include the afore-mentioned alcohol, cigarettes, and medications, as well as: environmental agents, such as pesticides, lead, and organic solvents; diseases, such as chickenpox and genital herpes; and other agents, such as radiation.

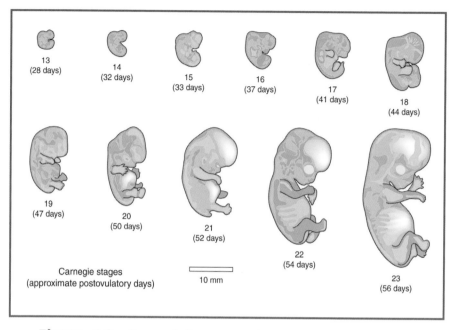

13
(28 days)

14
(32 days)

15
(33 days)

16
(37 days)

17
(41 days)

18
(44 days)

19
(47 days)

20
(50 days)

21
(52 days)

22
(54 days)

Carnegie stages
(approximate postovulatory days)

10 mm

23
(56 days)

Figure 1.3   Some of the stages that make up human embryonic development are illustrated here. The first two weeks of human development (not shown) are known as pre-embryonic, and after eight weeks (56 days) the developing human is known as a fetus. Embryonic development involves many processes that give rise to the distinctly human appearing fetus.

Although the mechanisms by which some teratogens can affect normal development are understood, others are not. For example, how thalidomide disrupts normal development is still largely a mystery. The degree of progress made within the field of developmental biology, however, has provided many insights into the mechanisms that control normal development.

The remainder of this book will focus on the events that are involved in healthy human development. The general organization of this book mirrors the timing of the developmental events that will be discussed, beginning with the earliest developmental events that occur and highlighting several of the events that take place as the embryo develops human form (Figure 1.3). The complexity of the events that occur during this time period are vast and beyond the scope of this book; however, the material that will be covered should serve as an introduction and overview of some of the more significant and well understood events.

2

What Is Development?

Before discussing many of the actual events that are involved in human development, the question of "what is development?" should be addressed. As was discussed in the previous chapter, development is the process, or processes, where a single cell becomes a multicellular organism. During that time, a single cell divides many times to produce many cells. These cells undergo a limitless number of events at the cellular, molecular, and genetic levels to shape this collection of cells into the form of a human. Development, then, depends on a limitless number of events at the cellular, molecular, and genetic levels. These events, in turn, combine into a complex array of pathways and processes that interact together in the correct place and with the correct timing to produce the mechanisms that construct the embryo. Because these pathways and processes are made up of combinations of events, their disruption, by an agent such as thalidomide, can potentially result in a domino effect that can greatly affect the development of the embryo as a whole.

As recently as 300 years ago, it was believed that humans developed by a process known as preformation. The basis of this mechanism is that individuals develop from fully formed, but extremely miniature, versions of themselves that are present in **germ cells**. The term "germ cells" refers to sperm and ova or eggs. According to preformation, every person who would ever exist has existed since the beginning of the human race. These people are somewhat like Russian nesting dolls where each germ cell contains a miniature human whose germ cells, in turn, contain even more miniature humans and so on. Development, then, would be characterized by the growth and unfolding of these miniature humans. It was unclear, however, as to whether the sperm or the ova contained this miniature human. This created factions among the preformationists. Ovists believed that organisms originated from the egg, and spermists believed they originated from the sperm.

As microscopes improved and the field of cell biology advanced, it became clear that development involved a great deal more than preformation. Making use of more powerful microscopes, embryologists learned more about human development. Kaspar Friedrich Wolff (1733–1794) observed that during chick development, embryonic structures, such as the heart and kidneys, look very different from the adult structures into which they develop. If preformation were the mechanism by which development was proceeding, embryonic and adult structures would appear identical, only differing in their size. Wolff also observed that structures such as the heart actually developed anew in each embryo. The view of development that Wolff observed, where structures arise progressively, is known as **epigenesis** (a Greek word meaning "upon formation"). Interestingly, the idea of epigenesis as the over-riding mechanism of development was first recognized and supported by the Greek philosopher Aristotle (384–322 B.C.).

THE FIVE GENERAL STEPS OF DEVELOPMENT: GROWTH, CELL DIVISION, DIFFERENTIATION, MORPHOGENESIS, AND PATTERNING

During human fetal development, from the beginning of the ninth week of development until birth, growth is essentially the major mechanism that is occurring. The fetus greatly resembles a miniature adult, although some structures, such as the head, are further advanced in growth than others. During this time of development, the fetus grows from a mere one inch in length to an average length of 20 inches. Before this time,

the exception of the mouse, undergo development outside of the mother, in eggs, making it possible to observe their development under a microscope as it is actually occurring.

It is important to remember that despite the great differences between organisms such as a nematode, a fish, and a human, there is also a great deal in common. All of these organisms are animals, and all animals share degrees of similarity. For example, the appearances of the embryos of a fish, a bird, and a human are remarkably similar (Figure 2.1). Based on this, it is clear that a great deal of information may be gleaned by studying the most seemingly unlikeliest of creatures. Furthermore, these less obvious choices may actually provide greater insights into human biology than the obvious would.

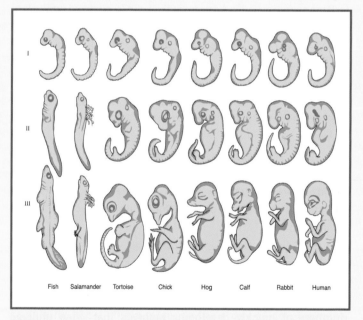

Figure 2.1 *The development of many diverse animals, including humans, share similarities at the level of development, as is illustrated here. By studying these model organisms, we can gain a better understanding of our own development.*

The zygote, which is a single cell, is microscopic in size. The human baby is estimated to consist of 10 trillion cells. For a single-celled zygote to develop into this multicellular organism it has to undergo cell division, also known as **mitosis**. Mitosis involves cellular reproduction, where one cell divides into two cells, those two cells can, in turn, divide to give rise to four cells, and so on.

The process of cell division can give rise to a vast number of cells. In general, however, mitosis gives rise to daughter cells that are identical to the parent. If mitosis and growth were the only mechanisms available to development, the result would be a large mass of identical and uniform cells. The human body is not made of a mass of identical cells, however. It is estimated that the human body is made up of more than 200 different kinds of cells. Some examples of the different kinds of cells that make up a human include skin cells, muscle cells, nerve cells or neurons, blood cells, and **fibroblasts** or connective tissue cells (Figure 2.2). These different kinds of cells vary in their size, shape, and function. The process by which cells become physically and functionally different and unique is called differentiation.

Differentiation, together with growth and cell division, still does not represent the complete story of development. These processes can give rise to a large mass of cells that are capable of doing different things (blood cells carry oxygen while muscle cells are capable of expanding and contracting, for example); however, they are not involved in imparting the physical appearance upon the developing embryo. The actual physical appearance of the embryo is dependent on two mechanisms: **morphogenesis** and **patterning**.

Morphogenesis is the process of the embryo, or regions of the embryo, taking on shape and form in three dimensions. If you look at your hand, you observe a great deal of form that came about as a result of morphogenesis. Each finger has its own unique shape and form as does the hand itself. The form

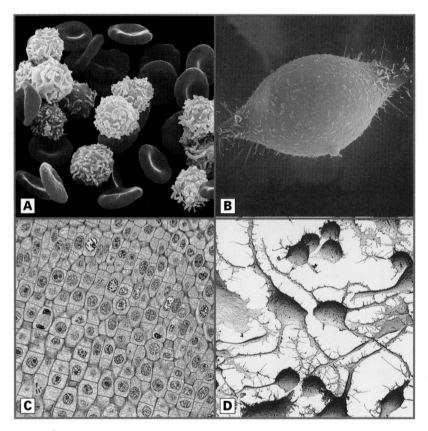

Figure 2.2 Cells in the body have many different shapes and properties. Some examples of differentiated cell types are shown here: A) disc-shaped red blood cells and round white blood cells B) a connective tissue cell, or fibroblast C) skin cells D) nerve cells or neurons.

of fingers is different from that of toes because of variations in the morphogenetic pathways during the development of each of these different digits.

The other process used to impart appearance on the embryo is called patterning. Patterning is the process used to lay down, or map out, the body plan. This process includes establishing the axes of the embryo, such as which side is dorsal (front) and which side is ventral (back); which end is anterior (the location of the head), versus the posterior location; and which side is left and which is right. Patterning also involves establishing the location of the limbs along the anterior-posterior axis of body and the order of fingers and toes on the hands and feet.

CONNECTIONS

The processes of growth, cell division, differentiation, patterning, and morphogenesis are all involved during the developmental process. Growth and cell division are often intimately linked as often an increase in the number of cells directly results in an increase in size. Differentiation is the process where cells take on specific fates that will dictate the functions these cell play in the organism. Patterning is the process that organizes structures and groups of cells in the organism. Morphogenesis is the process that confers shape and form upon the organism. Although development is clearly very complex, these five processes are, in very general terms, used in combination to produce a human. In addition, these same basic processes are used by virtually all forms of multicellular life on this planet, including all animals and plants, as they undergo development.

3

The Starting Point of Development: The Cell

Humans begin as a single cell, or zygote, when the sperm and egg join. The zygote divides to give rise to two cells that are virtually identical to each other. These two daughter cells are then capable of each dividing to give rise to four cells, which can then, in turn, divide again. This process allows for an exponential increase in cell number as each round of cell division can potentially double the number of cells produced by the previous division. This type of mechanism involving exponential cell division can be repeated however many times as required to yield enough cells to build a human. Because of this mechanism's fundamental importance to development, it is clear that the cell can be considered to be the fundamental unit of life. Therefore, an understanding of the cell in terms of how it is constructed, organized, and functions is crucial to understanding human biology, including development. This chapter will provide a brief introduction to the organization and general mechanistic functions of a cell.

ORGANIZATION AND FUNCTIONS OF A TYPICAL CELL

In the previous chapter, a number of different kinds of human cells were introduced. Some examples of these different kinds of cells that make up a human include skin cells, muscle cells, nerve cells or neurons, blood cells, and fibroblasts or connective tissue cells. These cells represent but a few examples of the many kinds of differentiated cells that humans have. These cells have many common elements, but they also have elements that are only found in each type of cell. It is these specific elements that result in the differentiated appearance and function of the specialized cell type described earlier.

The elements that are common to most human cells are also common to many types of cells in other animals. For example, there are certain basal, or very general, mechanisms, such as obtaining nutrients and converting nutrients into energy, which cells must be able to perform to exist. Regardless of the type of cell or the type of organism that cells make up, this type of function will likely have to be performed. Furthermore, most cells, regardless of their type, actually use very well conserved and similar mechanisms to perform this function. This degree of commonality further reinforces why model organisms can be used to give insights into human biology. Of further interest is the observation that cells that perform similar functions, but in different organisms, are also remarkably similar. It would be virtually impossible to tell the difference between a specific cell type whether it be from a human, a mouse, or a fish, simply by looking at the cells under a microscope. A human muscle cell more closely resembles a fish muscle cell than any other kind of human cell such as a blood cell (and the human blood cell is virtually identical to a fish blood cell). Regardless, all of these cells share many elements that will now be examined.

A typical animal cell (Figure 3.1) is similar to a container filled with specific structures. It is this collection of structures that act together for the cell to function. The outer surface, or walls, of this container is known as the plasma membrane. The plasma membrane acts to separate the inside of the cell from its surroundings, much like the function of our skin. Contained within the cell are many structures, called organelles, which play important roles in the functions a cell performs. An **organelle**, meaning "little organ," is a structure

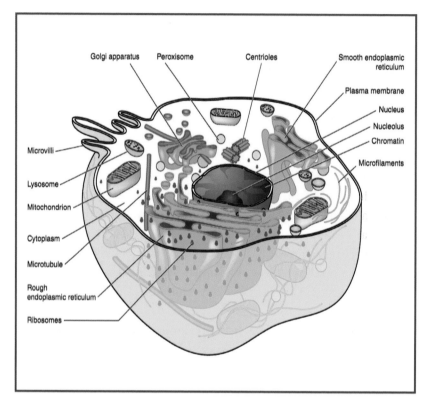

Figure 3.1 A diagrammatic representation of a typical animal cell is illustrated here. The general shapes and locations of the organelles such as the nucleus, endoplasmic reticulum, Golgi apparatus, and mitochondria are indicated.

in a cell that has a specific structure and function, much like the organs in an animal do. Organelles are generally surrounded by a membrane that is very similar, if not identical, to the plasma membrane surrounding the cell. Like the plasma membrane, the function of the organelle's membrane is to separate the inside of the organelle from the rest of the environment inside of the cell.

The largest organelle is the **nucleus**, the genetic control center of the cell. It contains the **genome**, or the **DNA** that represents the blueprints for the cell. All of the processes within a cell are controlled by the nucleus, specifically by the DNA contained within the nucleus. DNA also represents the heritable material of the cell. This means that during cellular reproduction, each daughter cell inherits the same blueprints as the parent cell. This is important because the heritable nature of DNA ensures that each cell that makes up an organism will contain essentially the same blueprints.

Adjacent to the nucleus is the **endoplasmic reticulum**, a network of membranous, flattened sacs and tubes. The region of the endoplasmic reticulum closest to the nucleus is covered with **ribosomes**, giving it a rough appearance. This region is called the rough endoplasmic reticulum. Ribosomes are essentially molecular machines that are used to make proteins and are also found floating freely throughout the inside of the cell. The distal endoplasmic reticulum, or the region of this organelle furthest from the nucleus, does not have the ribosome covering and is, therefore, often called the smooth endoplasmic reticulum. The rough endoplasmic reticulum is the site of protein synthesis; the smooth endoplasmic reticulum is the site where the cell modifies proteins made in the rough endoplasmic reticulum. The smooth endoplasmic reticulum is also the site of synthesis of **steroids**, **fatty acids**, and **phospholipids**, which are the major components that make up the cell's membranes.

The **Golgi apparatus** is also made up of flattened membranous sacs. The Golgi apparatus stores, modifies, and packages proteins that have been produced in the endoplasmic reticulum and that will eventually be delivered to some other location within or outside of the cell.

Another organelle found in all animal cells is the **mitochondrion**. In fact, most cells contain many mitochondria. Mitochondria, often called the "power plants" of the cell, provide energy for the cell. They are long oval structures that are surrounded by an outer membrane and an inner membrane that is folded in upon itself. These folds are called cristae and the space inside of the mitochondrion is called the matrix. Molecules, such as sugars, fatty acids, and **amino acids**, are taken up by the mitochondria and converted into energy through a series of chemical reactions. These chemical reactions make use of the oxygen obtained during respiration; therefore, these reactions are referred to as oxidation reactions. During these oxidation reactions, larger molecules, such as sugars, are broken down into the relatively small molecules of carbon dioxide (CO_2) and water (H_2O). As these larger molecules are broken down, the energy that was originally holding the larger molecules together is released and harvested for use by the cell. This energy is typically transferred to and stored in bonds that hold molecules called **activated carriers** together. An example of an activated carrier molecule is **adenosine triphosphate (ATP)**.

In addition to these relatively large organelles, cells also generally contain a large number of small membrane-bound organelles called vesicles. These structures essentially act as storage units inside of the cell. They can be used to transport materials within the cell, and they can also be used to store waste products of the cell. Peroxisomes, for example, are vesicles that contain digestive enzymes that are used to break down harmful or toxic materials inside of the cell. It is important to keep these enzymes separated from the rest of the cell, in these vesicles, so as not to digest the cell.

The cell also contains a network of tubular and filamentous proteins that make up the **cytoskeleton** of the cell. The cytoskeleton not only provides a protein scaffolding that acts as a support for the cell and its shape, but it also is used by the cell to move and to move molecules within the cell.

THE GENOME: THE BLUEPRINT OF THE CELL

The description of the cell and the major components that make it up illustrate that a typical cell is a complex collection of components that act together for the cell to function. All of these processes are controlled by the nucleus, specifically by the

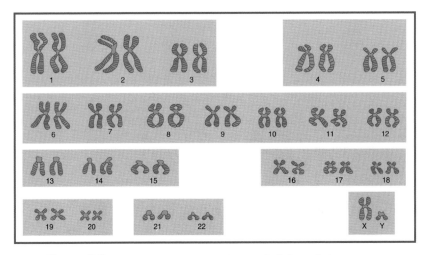

Figure 3.2 A human karyotype, or an image of a full set of chromosomes from a cell (46) that are arranged according to their size and shape, is shown here. Notice that the majority of the chromosomes are organized as pairs with the only exception being the X and Y chromosomes. Females have in their cells a pair of X chromosomes, while cells from a male have a single X chromosome and a single Y chromosome.

DNA contained within the nucleus. The DNA contained within the human nucleus is spread among 46 separate strands of DNA, or **chromosomes**. These 46 chromosomes are divided into 2 pairs of 23 and each set of 23 chromosomes represents a genome (Figure 3.2). With the exception of germ cells, human cells typically contain two genomes (one genome is obtained from the mother and one from the father,) and are therefore called **diploid**. This characteristic of genomic DNA is also a reflection of its heritable nature. This nature of DNA ensures that children will represent a combination of the genomes of each parent. It is for this reason that children have physical traits of both parents and that grandchildren have physical traits of each grandparent.

The heritable nature of DNA is an extremely important aspect that this genetic material must be capable of as it ensures that not only every cell in a particular organism will have virtually identical instructions to follow, but also that children will represent a combination of instructions from each parent. In addition to this, DNA must also be able to direct the operations of the cell and to direct the intercellular interactions. These roles of DNA are primarily accomplished by it acting as instructions for making **proteins**. Proteins are molecules that carry out the majority of cellular functions. The importance of proteins in relationship to the functions of the cell is reflected in

CLONING BY NUCLEAR TRANSFER

Recently, the possibility of producing organisms either asexually or by cloning has received a great deal of media attention. In 1997, biologists in Scotland announced the birth of Dolly the sheep. Dolly was the first mammal cloned from an adult cell. The implications of Dolly have been far reaching, particularly because the technique used to clone her can potentially be applied to many organisms including humans. Sexual reproduction involves combining genetic information from two parents, thus creating a unique individual. Cloning, or asexual reproduction, involves the production of an organism that is genetically identical to an individual that already exists. The technique used to produce Dolly is called "nuclear transplantation" or "somatic cell nuclear transfer."

This technique of nuclear transfer or transplantation requires two key ingredients: an egg cell and the genetic material from a somatic cell. A somatic cell is any cell that makes up an organism with the exception of the cells that give rise to gametes, or sperm and eggs. The actual nuclear transfer involves removing the genetic material, or the nucleus, from the egg cell and replacing it with donor genetic material that has been removed from a somatic cell of an individual. Instead of genetic material from two individual parents being combined to produce a zygote, a zygote is instead produced that contains the genetic material of only one individual. After the donor genetic material has been introduced into the enucleated egg cell (nucleus has been removed), this cell is stimulated to begin the observation that proteins make up the majority of the dry mass of the cell. Some of the functions that proteins execute in the cell include: constructing the cytoskeleton, which gives the cell its shape and the ability to move; acting as enzymes to catalyze the majority of the chemical reactions that occur in the cell; acting as channels and pumps embedded in cell membranes to control the passage of molecules into the cell and into organelles; and acting as external and internal signals and

development either chemically or by an electric shock. The embryo that begins to develop can potentially grow and develop for a number of days in the laboratory. Continued development requires that this pre-embryo be implanted into a surrogate mother, however. The individual who develops from this embryo, instead of representing a combination of the genetic traits of two parents, will be virtually genetically identical to the individual who provided the donor genetic material.

The question of how this technique can benefit society remains to be answered. Human cloning can prove to be beneficial. It has been proposed that this technique can potentially be used to help couples that are infertile to have children. This technique can also potentially be used to clone a child who has died. In addition, it can help people who suffer from degenerative diseases such as Alzheimer's disease, Parkinson's disease, Huntington's disease, and ALS (Lou Gehrig's disease). Cloning can potentially help treat diseases by creating a clone of the individual suffering from the diseases, and then using the embryo created as a source of stem cells to treat the disease (stem cells and their uses are discussed in greater detail in the next chapter). However, the process of cloning is incredibly inefficient, and much research still needs to be done to perfect this technique. For example, Dolly was the only clone born from a study that began with 277 zygotes created by nuclear transfer.

messages that allow cells to communicate with other cells and for cellular components of a particular cell to communicate with each other. Clearly, proteins play an important role in cellular functions. The question of the relationship between DNA, acting as the instructions, and proteins, implementing these instructions, remains to be discussed however.

FROM GENOTYPE TO PHENOTYPE: FOLLOWING THE BLUEPRINT

To understand how DNA acts as the blueprint for the cell and organism requires some understanding of the molecular nature of DNA. In a cell, DNA typically exists as two strands of molecules that wind around each other to form a double helix structure (Figure 3.3). Each strand of DNA is made up of a long chain of molecules called nucleotides. Nucleotides are made up of three subunits: a base joined to a deoxy-ribose sugar molecule that, in turn, is joined to a phosphate group. Nucleotides are joined together in such a way that deoxy-ribose sugars and phosphate groups form alternating units that make up a flexible, ribbon-like backbone. Extending away from this backbone are the bases. There are four different bases that make up DNA: adenine, cytosine, guanine, and thymine, commonly abbreviated A, C, G, and T, respectively. An important characteristic of these bases is that they are able to interact with each other in certain combinations. Adenine and thymine are able to bind to one another as are guanine and cytosine. These interactions hold the two strands of DNA together to form the double helix and make up the rungs holding the strands of DNA together as seen in Figure 3.3. An adenine on one strand binds to a thymine on the opposite, or complementary, strand, and a guanine on one strand binds to a cytosine on the complementary strand.

The sequence of bases along a strand of DNA is also able to code for the production of protein, thus enabling DNA to direct the operations of the cell. Regions of DNA that are able

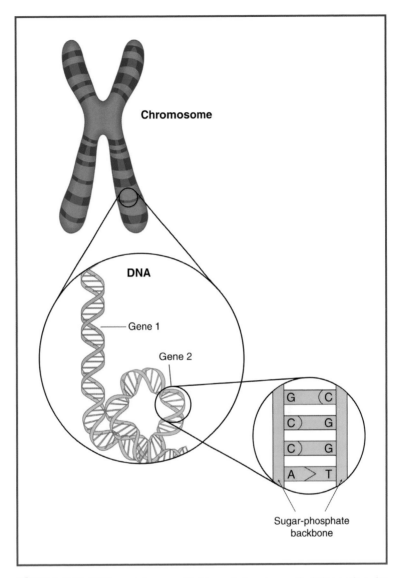

Figure 3.3 DNA contains a cell's blueprint and genetic information. Its structure and organization is illustrated here. Chromosomes are made up of a double strand of DNA that has a double helical structure. The flexible ribbons of the DNA strands represent the sugar phosphate backbone, and the interactions that hold the two strands together are a result of a base on each strand pairing with a complementary base on the opposite strand. The base pairings are represented as the rungs holding the strands together.

this RNA is principally used as a message, it is often called messenger RNA, or mRNA.

The next step of the process of following the instructions of the gene is called translation. This process takes the mRNA molecule and decodes the information in the four-letter (A, C, G, U) nucleotide language. The molecular machines that decode this information are ribosomes. The translation process involves a ribosome binding to an mRNA molecule. The ribosome moves along the mRNA and, following specific coding rules, translates the information from the four-letter nucleotide language to another language that contains twenty letters. This language is that of the protein, and the letters are amino acids. Proteins are made up of chains of twenty different amino acids. Different proteins are made up of different sequences of the twenty amino acids, and based on their differences in sequence, the proteins are able to perform different functions. Different proteins are able to perform virtually all of the cell's functions and to account for the cell's appearance. By extending this, and considering that animals and plants are large collections of cells, proteins, therefore, account for the functions and appearance of the organism. The function and appearance of an organism is called the phenotype. Thus, the information coded for in genes, or the genotype, controls the functions and appearance, or the phenotype, of the organism through the processes of transcription and translation.

CONNECTIONS

A typical cell is a complex collection of components that act together for the cell to function. The endoplasmic reticulum produces materials needed by the cell, the Golgi apparatus sends these materials to where they are needed, and the mitochondria provide the energy. In addition there are structures that act as storage containers and other structures that act as scaffolding and enable cell movements. All of these processes are controlled by the nucleus, specifically by the DNA contained within the nucleus. Cellular functions are controlled by specific regions of DNA called genes that collectively represent the genotype. The genotype controls the appearance and functions of the cell, or the phenotype, via two processes: transcription of an RNA copy of a gene and the subsequent translation of this RNA copy into protein.

It is the process of development that extends the cellular relationship between genotype and phenotype to construct an organism. During development, different cells express different sets of genes. This differential gene expression can lead to developmental events such as differentiation, patterning, and morphogenesis. Differential expression of subsets of genes in a cell can also result in that cell entering mitosis. In the next chapter, this extension of cellular events to construct an embryo will be discussed in more detail.

4

The First Steps to Multicellularity

In the last chapter, the organization of a basic cell was introduced. Also discussed were some of the basic mechanisms that generally take place in every cell, essentially in order for a cell to operate normally. These mechanisms were associated with specific organelles, such as the nucleus acting as the genetic control center of the cell. The concepts of transcription and translation were also introduced as the two processes that allow the genotype, or the DNA of the cell, to control the phenotype, or the appearance of the cell. Many of these concepts that were introduced will appear throughout this book. Understanding them will be important because they will form a basis for more widespread developmental mechanisms. In other words, to understand how development is occurring at the level of the organism will require an understanding of what is happening at both the molecular and cellular levels in that organism.

FERTILIZATION

The zygote, the first human cell in the process of development, forms when a sperm cell from the father fertilizes an oocyte, or egg cell, from the mother. Sperm and oocytes are specialized germ cells that differ from cells that make up the body of a human, or **somatic cells**, in that they are not **diploid**. Sperm and oocytes are **haploid**. This means that these germ cells reproduce using a specialized type of cell division called meiosis, which divides the genetic information in half. Most human cells are diploid; they contain two genomes or, in other words, two copies of the genetic information. The 46 chromosomes that make up the diploid genetic complement of a human cell are actually pairs of 23 different chromosomes. One of the chromosomes that makes up a particular pair comes from the mother and the other chromosome that is its twin comes from the father. Thus, when germ cells are produced, it must be in such a way that the genetic information is cut in half, so that they contain only one copy of each chromosome. After fertilization takes place, the zygote has the correct number of 46 chromosomes in the correct quantities to be able to develop into a diploid human. Furthermore, it is because of this that children inherit traits from each parent.

The process leading up to fertilization typically involves a number of sperm cells coming into contact with the much larger egg cell, or **oocyte** (Figures 4.2a and 4.2b). The oocyte is surrounded by a protective covering called the **zona pellucida**. When a sperm comes into contact with the oocyte, the tip of the sperm head, the **acrosome**, releases an enzyme that digests a region of the zona pellucida. This forms a path through the zona pellucida for the sperm to pass through. Once the sperm makes its way though the zona pellucida, it comes into contact with the cell membrane surrounding the oocyte, and the membranes surrounding the sperm and oocyte cells fuse. This fusion of sperm and oocyte membranes allows the nucleus of the sperm to enter the oocyte. The fusion of a single sperm with the oocyte also produces a change in the zona pellucida that prevents any other sperm from entering. Fertilization is considered to be complete when the haploid nucleus from the sperm fuses with the haploid egg nucleus. This fusion creates the diploid nucleus of the zygote.

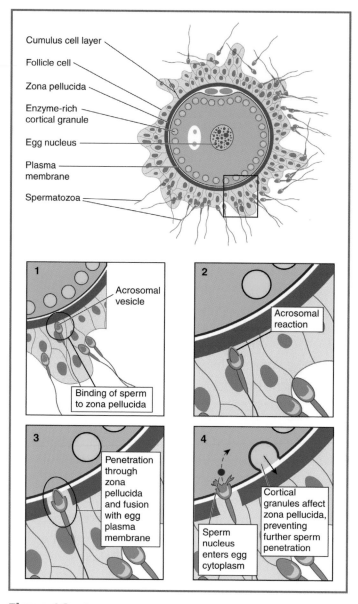

Figure 4.2a Several steps take place as a sperm comes into contact with and fertilizes an oocyte. First the sperm binds to the zona pelludica of the egg. Then the acrosome releases a special enzyme that digests the zona pelludica, allowing the sperm to enter the egg. Finally, cortical granules prevent any additional sperm from penetrating the zona pelludica.

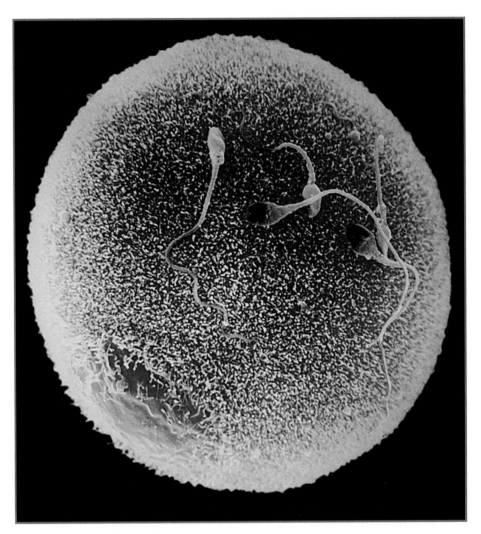

Figure 4.2b Shown here is a scanning electron micrograph of an oocyte being fertilized. Note that although several sperm are competing for a chance to fertilize the egg, only one can enter.

CLEAVAGE

After fertilization, the zygote will begin to undergo development. This single cell will eventually give rise to every cell that will make up the person it will develop into. During the first four days after fertilization, the stage known as cleavage, the principle developmental mechanism that is being employed is cell division, or mitosis. The process of cleavage involves a series of cell divisions that are not accompanied by any growth. Essentially what is occurring is that the relatively large zygote is subdivided into a number of smaller cells whose combined size is approximately the same as the zygote. During this time, approximately five cell divisions occur, resulting in 32 cells. These 32 cells are essentially identical to one another and are all clustered together in a single mass. This mass of cells is called the **morula**, which literally means "little mulberry" and is based on the clustered appearance of the cells at this stage (Figure 4.3). This process is fueled by nutrients present in the original oocyte. These nutrients are not sufficient, however, as a supply for the entire developmental process. To obtain nutrients to support subsequent development, the pre-embryo will ultimately have to attach to the mother.

DEVELOPMENT OF THE
EXTRA-EMBRYONIC TISSUES

Cleavage, the development of the morula, and the subsequent attachment to the mother is commonly referred to as the "pre-embryonic" stage of development. Many of the cells of the pre-embryo will not actually contribute to the embryo. The cells that do not contribute to the actual embryo will instead form the extra-embryonic tissues, such as the placenta. Around the fourth day after fertilization, cells of the pre-embryo continue to divide, but also begin to undergo differentiation and morphogenesis. During the next several days, cells present on the outside of the pre-embryo will begin to differentiate, or will begin to take on specific fates. In addition, cells of the pre-embryo will begin to make morphogenic movements, as the shape of the pre-embryo changes from the mulberry shape of the morula to

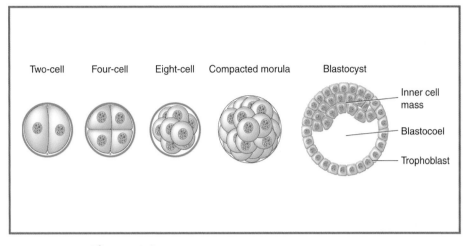

Two-cell   Four-cell   Eight-cell   Compacted morula   Blastocyst

Inner cell mass

Blastocoel

Trophoblast

Figure 4.3 Pre-embryonic development involves several steps of cell division. The process of cleavage involves five synchronous cell divisions that give rise to a 32-cell morula. The cells of the morula will continue to divide and will rearrange themselves into a more rounded and hollow ball-like shape called the blastocyst.

a more rounded ball-like shape. This ball of cells is called the **blastocyst**. If one were to cut this blastocyst, so that it could be observed in a cross section, three distinct regions would be observed. Inside the blastocyst, there is a hollow cavity, the **blastocoel**, as well as a collection of cells called the **inner cell mass**. The cell layer that makes up the outer sphere of the blastocyst is called the **trophoblast**.

The cells of the trophoblast mediate the implantation of the blastocyst into the uterine wall of the mother. Implantation takes place during the second week of development. This process begins when the blastocyst comes into contact with the endometrium, or lining of the uterus. This lining cycles in thickness during the menstrual cycle of the female and is at its thickest during the time of the cycle that is most prone to pregnancy. When the blastocyst comes into contact with the endometrium, the trophoblast cells surrounding the blastocyst secrete digestive enzymes that break down the endometrial cells. This breakdown creates a path that allows the blastocyst to burrow into the endometrial lining.

After implantation, cells of the trophoblast continue to divide and differentiate and will give rise to the **chorion**, the outermost layer of cells surrounding the implanted embryo. This layer of cells produces hormones to support the early pregnancy. The chorion also produces and releases digestive enzymes that break down the mother's endometrial cells and capillaries in the area surrounding the embryo. This digestion of capillaries leads to their rupture and the formation of cavities filled with blood in the vicinity of the embryo. The chorion also extends projections into these blood-filled cavities to allow the embryo to obtain nutrients and oxygen from them while excreting wastes. The structure that is formed by the chorion, its projections into the endometrium, and the endometrium itself are called the **placenta**.

THE EARLY EMBRYO:
THE INNER CELL MASS

The embryo develops from the inner cell mass of the blastocyst. At the stage of pre-embryonic development, the cells of the inner cell mass are essentially equivalent to each other. If the inner cell mass were to be divided, each cell or collection of cells that results has the potential to form an embryo. In fact, it is just such a division that can lead to the development of monozygotic, or identical, twins during development (Figure 4.4). These cells are often referred to as being **pluripotent** because any one of the cells that make up the inner cell mass has the capacity to form any type of human cell or tissue. The cells of the inner cell mass, during the first several weeks of development, are pluripotent largely because they have not differentiated into specific cells. After approximately the first two weeks of development, which largely involves the development of the

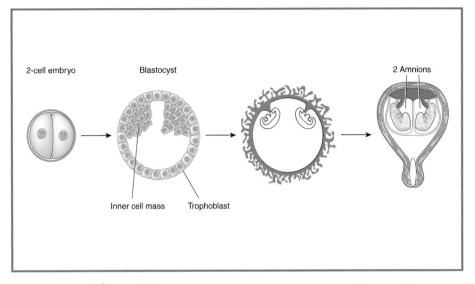

Figure 4.4 The division of the inner cell mass, illustrated here, can result in each half of the inner cell mass giving rise to an embryo. Such an event can lead to the development of monozygotic or identical twins.

extra-embryonic tissues, the inner cell mass begins a program of rapid growth, differentiation, and morphogenesis that lasts for approximately six weeks. This period of development beginning at the start of the third week and finishing near the end of the eighth week is when the developing human is called an embryo.

CONNECTIONS

Following fertilization, the zygote undergoes a number of cell divisions during a stage called cleavage. This process results in a mass of relatively uniform cells. The cells located on the outside of this mass become the trophoblast. This gives rise to the extra-embryonic tissues, such as the placenta, and thus plays an important role in implantation and the subsequent connection between embryo and mother that enables the embryo to obtain nutrients and dispose of wastes. Cells located in the inside of the pre-embryo will give rise to the inner cell mass which in turn will eventually give rise to every type of cell or tissue that makes up a human. Because of the

STEM CELLS

Human embryonic stem cells were first isolated in 1998 by James Thomson at the University of Wisconsin-Madison. Embryonic stem cells are obtained by harvesting cells from the inner cell mass of human blastocysts. This process destroys the pre-embryo, which is the principal reason that so much controversy surrounds embryonic stem cells. The primary source of blastocysts, from which embryonic stem cells may be obtained, is excess pre-embryos from in vitro fertilization (IVF). IVF is utilized to allow infertile couples to produce children. This technique involves removing a number of oocytes and sperm from the parents and mixing these germ cells in a dish in the laboratory. Typically, many oocytes are fertilized during this procedure, with only a subset of them being implanted into the mother. The remaining pre-embryos are generally frozen. If these frozen pre-embryos are never used, the parents may consent to donate them for research. Upon their isolation, these cells can be cultured in the laboratory potentially providing an indefinite supply.

With continued research, stem cells may become a very powerful tool that can be used to treat many human diseases, particularly degenerative diseases. The cells of the inner cell mass are pluripotent, or have the potential to become any cell type or tissue that is found in a human. Potential uses for embryonic stem cells are to treat diseases such as Alzheimer's disease, Parkinson's disease, Huntington's disease, ALS (Lou Gehrig's disease) as well as spinal cord injuries. Embryonic stem cells also have the potential to be used to treat diseases and injuries that result in damage to part of an organ or tissue. For example, a heart attack results in the death of a portion of the heart muscle. Possibly, stem cells can be injected into damaged or injured tissues and induced to differentiate to repair that tissue.

versatility of these cells, they have the potential to be powerful tools for research as well as for potentially treating a large number of diseases. In the next chapter, the early developmental events in the embryo will be examined.

5

The Developing Embryo

The previous chapter discussed the early developmental event that results in the implantation of the embryo into the uterine lining of the mother. Also discussed was the development of the inner cell mass. During pre-embryonic development, the inner cell mass soon begins to move down pathways and to take on specific fates that will ultimately give rise to the actual embryo.

During the second week after fertilization, as the trophoblast is involved in implantation, inside the blastocyst a thin layer of cells called the hypoblast delaminates from the inner cell mass (Figure 5.1). These cells migrate and divide to line the blastocoel, and the newly lined cavity is called the yolk sac. Like the trophoblast, the yolk sac is actually considered to be an extra-embryonic tissue. As development proceeds, the yolk sac will become an extension of the developing gut of the embryo. As the hypoblast is forming, the cells of the inner cell mass that remain, and do not contribute to the hypoblast, become known as the **epiblast**. During the time that the hypoblast is forming, another layer of cells delaminates from the epiblast. This occurs on the side of the epiblast that is opposite from the hypoblast. This forms a second cavity that will come to be filled with amniotic fluid. This fluid-filled amniotic cavity insulates the developing baby and protects it. Later in development, as the kidneys form, the fetus will urinate into the amniotic cavity where these wastes will then be removed through exchange with the mother via the extra-embryonic tissues. The band of cells that remains in the inner cell mass, and that is now

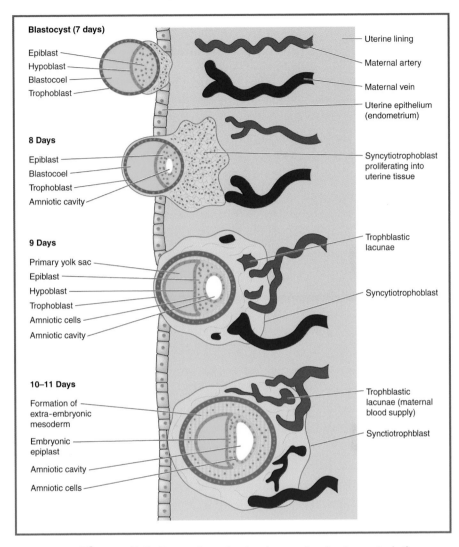

Figure 5.1 Pre-embryonic development prior to gastrulation is illustrated here. During this time, the trophoblast of the pre-embryo is involved in implanting into the uterine wall of the mother. As this is occurring, the cells of the inner cell mass continue to divide and will give rise to some extra-embryonic tissues as well as the embryo.

positioned between the yolk sac and amniotic cavity, is called the **embryonic disc**. This small collection of cells, approximately 0.1–0.2 millimeters in length, will give rise to the embryo.

GASTRULATION

The first major developmental event that the embryonic disc will undergo is **gastrulation**. During this process, the cells of the embryo undergo significant movements as they rearrange themselves. These movements ultimately lead to the establishment of the basic tissue types that will lead to the generation of the organs. Gastrulation also results in the establishment of the general layout of the body plan. Because of the broadly reaching impact on development, this stage is critically important for the continued development of the embryo. The significance of this developmental event is so great that the embryologist Lewis Wolpert has said, "it is not birth, marriage, or death, but gastrulation which is truly the most important time of your life."

Before gastrulation, the embryonic disc is essentially made up of two layers of cells and is referred to as being bilaminar (Figure 5.2). As gastrulation begins, cells on the surface of the disc that face away from the yolk sac begin moving toward the center line of the disc. These movements begin at one end of the disc. This end, or region, of the embryonic disc will eventually become the posterior end of the embryo.

As the cells from either side of the embryonic disc reach the center midline, they will collide. The midline where these collisions occur takes on an irregular appearance, relative to the rest of the surface of the embryonic disc. The sheets of cells converging at the midline of the embryonic disc give rise to a line running down the center of the embryonic disc. This line is called the **primitive streak**. These movements initiate at one end of the embryo. As cells collide at the midline to give rise to the primitive streak, cells are forced out along the axis being created along that midline. This causes the primitive streak to elongate along the axis of the midline towards the other end of the embryo. By analogy, the primitive streak is somewhat similar to toothpaste being squeezed out of a tube. Squeezing the tube of toothpaste causes the toothpaste

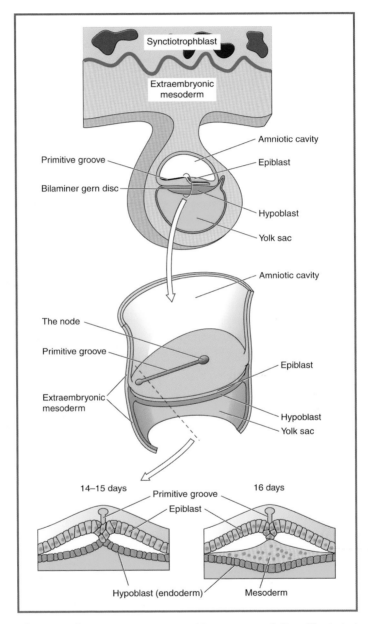

Figure 5.2 During the process of human gastrulation, illustrated here, the cells of the embryo undergo extensive movement and rearrangement to convert the bilaminar embryonic disc into a more complex structure made up of the three distinct germ layers.

particles to collide in the tube, and these collisions ultimately result in forcing some particles through the end of the tube.

In the embryo, cells colliding at the presumptive posterior end of the embryo, at the primitive streak, will force some cells to move perpendicular to their original direction of motion as they are squeezed together. This process causes the primitive streak to extend along the midline toward what will become the anterior end of the embryo. By the time this process is

STUDYING GASTRULATION

Studying gastrulation in humans is difficult because of the small size of the embryo during this process and because of the generally small number of human embryos that are available to study. A number of collections of preserved human embryos do exist, however, and these collections can be used to gain some insights into human development. In addition, early developmental events, such as cleavage, can be observed under a microscope during in-vitro fertilization procedures at fertility clinics, before the injection of the pre-embryos into the mother. Observing a gastrulating human embryo in this manner, however, is virtually impossible because gastrulation occurs after implantation and, thus, inside the uterus. What is known about gastrulation in humans, then, is gleaned from a combination of information from embryos in collections as well as from observing model organisms, such as mice and chick embryos. The cell movements that take place during gastrulation in the chick are remarkably similar to those that take place in mammals, including humans. Furthermore, these cell movements in chick embryos can actually be observed as they occur by cutting a window into the egg and observing development under a microscope. Using these observations from model organisms, the events that make up human gastrulation have been pieced together. Combining this data from different sources perfectly illustrates the power of utilizing model organisms to study development as was first introduced in chapter two.

completed, the anterior-posterior axis and the dorsal midline have been established.

At the front of the extending primitive streak, a structure called the **node** develops. The node, a knot-like structure, develops largely as a result of cells initially piling up in this region before being forced to move anteriorly. In organisms other than humans, the node is called Hensen's node, after its discoverer, the German anatomist and physiologist Viktor Hensen (1835–1924).

As cells move across the surface of the embryo and collide to form the extending primitive streak, cells at the primitive streak also pass into the disc. These cells move inward and pass through the primitive streak, which is now known as the **primitive groove**. Once the cells enter through the embryonic disc, they spread out between the two cell layers that make up the disc, the top epiblast and bottom hypo-blast. These two cell movements are the principle events associated with gastrulation. These cell movements transform the bilaminar embryonic disc into a more complex structure made up of three distinct layers. Collectively these populations of cells are known as the three germ layers: the ectoderm, the endoderm, and the mesoderm.

THE GERM LAYERS: ENDODERM, MESODERM, AND ECTODERM

The germ layers represent the three different cell types that will continue to differentiate during development to give rise to the more than 200 different types of cells that make up a human (Figure. 5.3). The endoderm lineage represents the inner-most layer of cells following gastrulation. These cells are the first to migrate through the primitive streak and the adult cells that they will give rise to include those that will make up the gut, the liver, and the lungs. The cells that migrate into the embryo later and that position themselves between the endoderm and surface layer become the mesoderm. The adult

ECTODERM
- Epidermis of skin (including hair, nails and sweat glands)
- Entire nervous system
- Lens, cornea, eye muscles (internal)
- Internal and external ear
- Epithelium of mouth, nose, salivary glands and anus
- Tooth enamel (in mammals)
- Epithelium of adrenal medulla and pineal gland

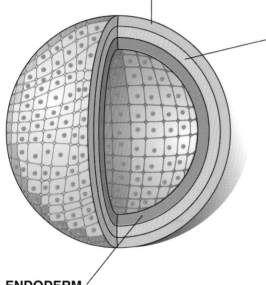

MESODERM
- Muscles
- Skeleton
- Blood
- Dermis of skin
- Endothelium of blood vessels
- Lymphoid tissue
- Middle ear
- Epithelium of kidneys
- Epithelium of gonads

ENDODERM
- Epithelium and glands of digestive tract
- Epithelium of lower respiratory tract
- Epithelium of urinary bladder
- Glandular epithelium (thyroid, parathyroid, pancreas, thymus)
- Epithelium of vagina and accessory sex structures

Figure 5.3 During development, cells form three germ layers. The positions of the three germ layers (ectoderm, mesoderm, and endoderm) relative to one another are shown. The ectoderm is the outermost layer, the mesoderm is the middle layer, and the endoderm is the innermost layer. Examples of the types of cells derived from each layer are also listed here.

cells that the mesoderm will give rise to include those that will make up the skeleton and skeletal muscle, the heart, the blood, and the kidneys. The cells that remain on the surface of the embryo become the ectoderm. The adult cells that this lineage of cells will give rise to include the skin and central nervous system.

CONNECTIONS

During the process of gastrulation, the cells of the embryo undergo significant morphogenetic movements that result in the establishment of the germ layers. The layers will continue to differentiate during development to give rise to more than 200 different types of cells that make up a human. Each of these germ layers is positioned in a manner consistent with the body plan of a human. The ectoderm which gives rise to the skin is positioned on the outer surface of the embryo. Beneath the ectoderm, the mesoderm is positioned where it will give rise to cells such as those giving rise to muscle and bone. The mesoderm overlays the endoderm, the lineage that will give rise to the digestive system. During this time, the future axes also become established. Thus, after gastrulation, much of the future body plan of the developing human has been mapped out. The next chapter will focus on how the layout of the body is further refined and how the ectodermal lineage gives rise to the central nervous system.

6

The Beginnings of the Central Nervous System

In the previous chapter, gastrulation, the first major developmental event that the embryonic disc will undertake, was discussed. During this process, the cells of the embryo undergo significant morpho-genetic movements that result in the establishment of the three germ layers. If one considers the relationship between the positions that the germ layers take up following gastrulation and the eventual fates of the cells of each of the germ layers, it makes a lot of sense in terms of the human body plan. The external appearance of this body plan is essentially made up of three axes: the anterior-posterior axis runs from head (the anterior) to tail (the posterior); the dorsal-ventral axis runs from front (ventral) to back (dorsal); and the final of the three axes runs from right to left. The discussion of gastrulation in the previous chapter described how this developmental event can actually contribute to the establishment of both the anterior-posterior and dorsal-ventral axes. Gastrulation also, and significantly, defines the internal organization of the body. If one imagines what a cross section through a human might look like in a very general sense, it would likely look something like the image shown in Figure 6.1. Running through the body, along the anterior-posterior axis, is

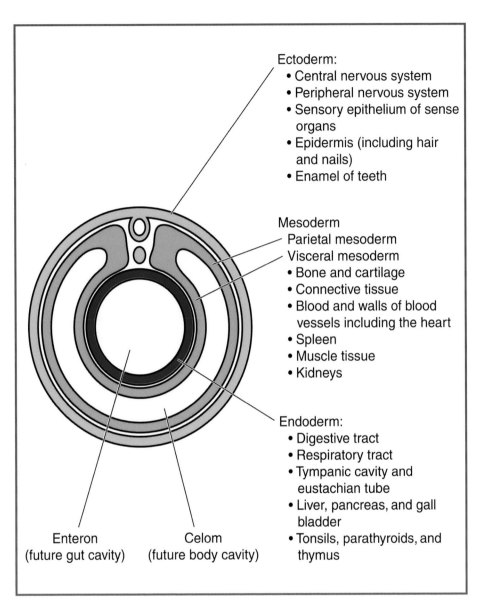

Figure 6.1 A diagrammatic representation showing the relative positions of the three germ layers and their derivatives is shown here. The enteron and celom will form the gut and body cavities, respectively. The ectoderm will form the central and peripheral nervous systems, as well as skin cells (epidermis). The mesoderm will form many essential organs, such as the bone, blood, heart, spleen, and kidneys. The endoderm will form the remaining organs as well as the digestive and respiratory tracts.

the gut. The gut is essentially a tube that runs from the mouth, through the digestive system and to the anus. The lining of the gut and the structures associated with it such as the stomach, intestines, and liver are all derived from the endoderm. Immediately surrounding the endodermal derivatives in the body is the musculature, the skeleton, and the circulatory system (the heart, blood vessels, and blood), or derivatives of the mesoderm. In terms of gastrulation, this makes sense as this process places the mesoderm immediately above the endoderm. Finally the cells that surround the mesodermal and endodermal derivatives come from the ectoderm. Just as it makes sense that the mesoderm would surround the endoderm because of what is known concerning gastrulation, so does the ectoderm or the germ layer present on the surface following gastrulation and giving rise to the skin, which represents the surface surrounding the body.

NEURULATION

The ectoderm, in addition to giving rise to the skin, also gives rise to the central nervous system. This latter ectodermal derivative is not as easy to reconcile with the cellular rearrangements associated with gastrulation. The reason for this is because **neurulation**, or the early development of the central nervous system, involves additional cellular movements. The process of neurulation forms the neural tube, a structure that runs along the anterior-posterior axis on the dorsal side of the embryo. This tube will eventually give rise to the brain, anteriorly, and the spinal cord, posteriorly.

The process of neurulation actually begins, to a certain extent, while gastrulation is occurring. During gastrulation, cells migrate through the entire length of the primitive groove to take up their positions as one of the germ layers. The subset of cells that migrate through the anterior region of the primitive streak, the node, are unique in that they will give rise to a specialized structure called the **notochord**. The notochord is a transient rod-like structure of cells that runs along the anterior-posterior axis of the embryo and lies beneath the developing central nervous system. The notochord releases molecular signals that instruct the overlying ectoderm to change, or begin to differentiate, into neural ectoderm. The ectodermal cells that are initially induced by the notochord in this manner are called the **neural plate**.

In response to this induction, the cells that make up the neural plate take on a distinctly elongated and columnar appearance. The neural plate subsequently folds inward (Figure 6.2) while the non-neural ectodermal cells on either side of the neural plate move toward the center. These non-neural ectodermal cells from either side of the neural plate will continue converging toward one another until they meet and join. This results in a layer of ectoderm overlying a tube formed from the neural plate folding inward then being pinched together along the dorsal side. This tube is called the neural tube and will eventually give rise to the brain and spinal cord as well as many of the various types of neurons, or nerve cells, that are present in the body. The closure of the neural tube as the overlying ectoderm converges and fuses above it does not occur simultaneously along the entire anterior-posterior axis of the developing embryo. In mammals, including humans, the neural tube initiates its closure at a number of locations along the anterior-posterior axis. From these points where its closure is initiated, the neural tube closes in opposite directions along the anterior-posterior axis until it is entirely enclosed.

This process is similar to pinching a zipper bag along the seal at a number of places and then continuing to seal the rest of the bag from these regions. Examples do exist of defects occurring during the process of neural tube closure in humans. The human congenital malformation spina bifida is

(continued on page 66)

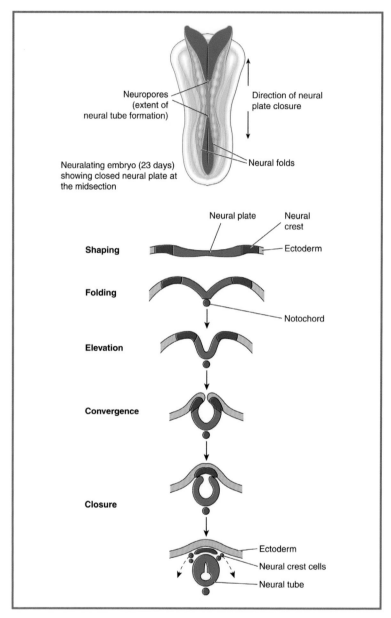

Figure 6.2 Neurulation involves the folding inward and subsequent internalization of surface ectodermal cells. This process of cell movements results in the formation of the neural tube which will give rise to the central nervous system.

SPINA BIFIDA

Spina bifida (Latin for "divided spine") is one of the most commonly occurring congenital malformations in humans. It is estimated that approximately 10% of all people exhibit this birth defect, which involves delayed or improper closure of the neural tube. This defect also leads to abnormalities in the bone, muscle, and skin surrounding the brain and spinal cord. The most common and mildest form of this malformation, spina bifida occulta, results from the failure of a single vertebra to fuse dorsally. The only outwardly visible sign of this is a small tuft of hair or perhaps a small dimple over the affected vertebra. In addition, there is no pain or neurological defect associated with this form. A more severe form of this malformation, spina bifida cystica, is considerably less common. This form results when multiple vertebrae fail to fuse leading to the spinal cord bulging out into a skin-covered cyst on the outside of the body. This is typically accompanied by neurological disorders whose severity is dependent on the degree to which neural tissue bulges into the cyst.

Severe spina bifida can also accompany the related congenital malformation *anencephaly* (Greek for "not brain"). This malformation is lethal and infants suffering from it are either stillborn or die shortly after birth. Anencephaly, like spina bifida, results from the failure of the neural tube to close. Whereas spina bifida involves defects more posteriorly, anencephaly results from defects more anteriorly, specifically in the cephalic or brain region. This failure of the anterior neural tube to close during neurulation leads to the degeneration of the forebrain and the failure of the vault of the skull to form. Interestingly, studies have shown that more than half of the incidences of spina bifida and anencephaly in humans can be prevented by supplementing the diet of the pregnant woman with folic acid. For this reason, the Centers for Disease Control and Prevention recommends that all women of childbearing age take folic acid daily to reduce the risk of neural tube defects during pregnancy.

(continued from page 63)
just such an example of a birth defect that results from a failure of the neural tube to close.

NEURAL CREST:
THE FOURTH GERM LAYER?

The process of neurulation, in addition to giving rise to
the neural tube and central nervous system, also gives rise
to a population of cells known as the **neural crest**. When
the neural tube is formed by the pinching together of the
ectodermal cells lying on either side of the neural plate, a
collection of cells initially link the newly formed neural
tube and overlying ectoderm. It is these cells that initially
link and lie between the future central nervous system
and future epidermis or skin that becomes the neural crest.
Neural crest cells migrate extensively throughout the body
during development and also give rise to a large number of
cell types and structures. Interestingly, neural crest cells can
give rise to cell types not normally associated with being
derived from ectoderm (as the neural crest is). For example,
neural crest cells that come into being during the closure of
the anterior, or cranial region, of the neural tube give rise
to facial cartilage and bone as well as the smooth muscle of
the face, head, and neck. Other derivatives of the neural
crest include components of the peripheral nervous system,
components of the endocrine and paracrine systems, pig-
ment cells, and even components of the teeth. Because the
neural crest plays an important role in the development of
all vertebrates, including humans, it is sometimes referred
to as the fourth germ layer.

THE BRAIN

Before neurulation has completed, the anterior region of the
neural tube, which will give rise to the brain, is already undergoing significant further developmental events. At approximately

four weeks into development, the presumptive brain forms as three bulges in the anterior neural tube: the forebrain or **prosencephalon**; the midbrain or **mesencephalon**; and the hindbrain or **rhombencephalon** (Figure 6.3).

The forebrain will shortly give rise to the **optic vesicles**, which extend outward from each side. The forebrain will subdivide further into the anterior **telencephalon**, which will become the cerebrum, and the more posterior **diencephalon**, which will give rise to the **thalamus** and **hypothalamus**, the regions of the brain involved in emotions and conscious thought.

The midbrain will give rise to structures such as the optic lobes and tectum and control functions that relate to hearing and vision.

The hindbrain will come to control movements of the body as well as the vital automatic functions of the internal organs. The hindbrain, or rhombencephalon, like the forebrain, is further subdivided as well. During its development, the hindbrain takes on a segmental pattern, where each segment is called a **rhombomere**. Each rhombomere represents a separate developmental compartment so cells from one rhombomere cannot mix with cells from another, and each rhombomere has its own distinct developmental fate. The rhombomeres will give rise to the cranial nerves, which will carry signals from the brain to the muscles, receptors, and glands of the head, neck, and thoracic and abdominal cavities.

CONNECTIONS

The process of neurulation involves the involution of a region of the dorsal ectoderm, thus positioning a tube of cells just beneath the dorsal surface of the developing body. This neural tube will give rise to the central nervous system including the brain and spinal cord. As development proceeds, the posterior

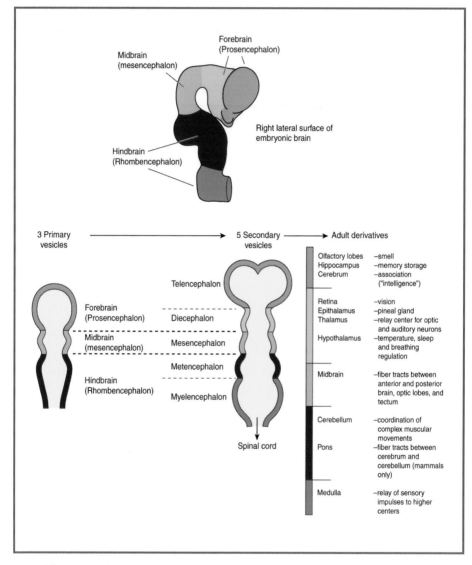

Figure 6.3 Development of the brain from the anterior end of the neural tube is illustrated here. The brain develops from three primary vesicles (the forebrain, midbrain, and hindbrain) that, in turn, will further subdivide into their adult derivatives. The three primary vesicles begin to form about four weeks into development.

neural tube will give rise to the spinal cord, and the mesoderm surrounding it will come to envelop it with a protective covering of bone in the form of vertebrae. The anterior region of the neural tube will develop into the different compartments of the brain that will be encased in a skull derived from mesoderm.

7

Establishing the Axes

The previous two chapters have primarily focused on questions of human development concerning morphogenesis and differentiation. These two developmental processes obviously play a very important role in the events associated with gastrulation and neurulation. Morphogenetic movements during both of these events rearrange the cells and shape of the developing embryo such that the embryo becomes consistent with the general plan of the body. As cells are being positioned in this manner, they are also beginning to take on more specificity in terms of their form and function. Cells positioned on the inside of the embryo embark down endodermal and mesodermal pathways. The ectodermal cells on the surface of the embryo initially seem destined to remain on the outside of the body and to make up cell types such as epidermis or skin. Neurulation then takes place, however, and positions a subset of these cells such that they will also give rise to the central nervous system, including the brain and spinal cord.

As the embryo is undergoing gastrulation, decisions are also being made concerning the establishment of the axes that make up the body plan. The position of the node of the primitive streak reflects the anterior end of the anterior-posterior axis of the embryo and, ultimately, the adult that it will develop into. In addition, the surface of the embryonic disc that will migrate through the primitive streak during gastrulation is destined to become the dorsal side of the embryo and adult. Thus, by the time that gastrulation is completed the anterior-posterior and dorsal-ventral axes are defined, although the actual mechanisms that define these axes have not been discussed in depth.

The establishment of the embryonic axes during early development is clearly important. These early decisions essentially establish and outline a very general layout for the developing body. These decisions establish which side is anterior and which is posterior, which side is dorsal and which is ventral, and which side is left and which is right. Subsequent developmental events will then position specific structures and tissues in relation to these axes. To accomplish this, however, additional information must be present that will guide specific developmental events and processes to the correct location along the established axes. In other words, the axes must be further refined such that regions along these axes are specified. For example, before limb development (which will be discussed in greater detail in the next chapter), information must be present to specify the precise position along the anterior-posterior axis of the trunk from which the arm or leg will grow. This positional information is specified along the anterior-posterior axis by a group of genes called the **Hox genes**.

HOX GENES PATTERN
THE ANTERIOR-POSTERIOR AXIS

In Chapter 2, the concept that many animals share common elements during their development was introduced. Because of this, biologists can study different organisms as model systems to gain a better understanding of human biology. The *Hox* genes are an excellent example of a group of genes that are found in many different kinds of animals and that perform a similar function in these different animals. Studying the functions of *Hox* genes in one animal is, therefore, likely to provide insights into the role of *Hox* genes in another animal. The *Hox* genes are a group of genes that were first discovered in the fruit fly, *Drosophila melanogaster.*

Drosophila has been used as a model organism to study many biological questions for more than a century. One of the advantages of *Drosophila* as a model is the availability of a large number of mutants. A number of *Drosophila* mutants are classified as being homeotic. A homeotic mutation is one that results in the transformation of the identity of one region of an organism into the identity of another region, and these types of mutations can be found in many types of organisms ranging from plants to animals. Two such *Drosophila* mutants are the *bithorax* and *antennapedia* mutant flies (Figure 7.1). In the *bithorax* mutant fly, the third thoracic segment takes on the second thoracic segment's identity. In this mutant, the third thoracic segment, which usually has a haltere (a small organ used for balance during flight), takes on the identity of the second thoracic segment, which has a wing. Thus, this mutation results in a fly with two sets of wings and no halteres instead of one set of wings and one set of halteres.

Similarly, in the *antennapedia* mutant, a region of the fly's head has taken on the identity of the fly's thorax, thus the fly has legs rather than antennae extending from its head. If these mutant flies are considered from a patterning point of view, they exhibit the transformation of the identity of one region of an organism into the identity of another region through alterations in the specification of positional information along the anterior-posterior axis. In the *bithorax* mutant, for example, the third thoracic segment takes on the identity of a more anterior segment and in the *antennapedia* mutant a region of the head takes on a more posterior identity. This suggests that the genes that are mutated in these homeotic

Figure 7.1 Certain genes control the formation of certain body parts in an organism. If this gene is mutated, development may be altered. This phenomenon was first observed in the common fruit fly *Drosophila melanogaster*. A normal (wild type) *Drosophila* is shown on the left. A *Drosophila* displaying the *antennapedia* mutatation is shown on the right. The *antennapedia Drosophila* mutant has legs replacing its antennae.

flies likely play some role in patterning the anterior-posterior axis of the fly.

The genes that are mutated in the *Drosophila* genome that lead to these homeotic alterations in the bodies of the adult flies are called homeotic genes, or *HOM* genes. There are actually eight different *HOM* genes in the *Drosophila* genome and each one is named for the homeotic mutation it leads to. Thus, the *antennapedia* gene when mutated, leads to the transformation of the antennae of the fly into legs. Similarly, the *ultrabithorax* gene, when mutated, causes the third thoracic segment of the fly to take on the identity of the second one and a fly with two sets of wings instead of one arises. The

MUTATIONS

Mutations result from alterations in the nucleotide sequence of the genome. Mutations can arise anywhere along a chromosome including in the coding region of a gene or in regulatory regions that direct the expression of a gene. Chapter 3 introduced the concept that the nucleotide sequence of DNA represents the blueprints that direct the actions and functions of a cell and by extension the organism made up of such cells. Changes, or mutations, in the nucleotide sequence will then alter these blueprints, thus also altering cellular processes. The effect on the organism by mutations can vary. A mutation can have absolutely no effect on the organism. Conversely, mutations can have a significant impact. For example, a single nucleotide change in the human hemoglobin gene is the cause of sickle cell disease. In addition, mutations in genes that control cell division can often lead to cancer. Mutations can also alter the outward appearance of an organism. For example, mutations in the human fibroblast growth factor receptor *FGFR1* gene causes Pfeiffer syndrome which is characterized by limb defects and abnormalities in the shape of the face and skull.

Mutations can be incredibly valuable tools with which to study developmental biology. If a gene is mutated leading to a developmental defect or an alteration in the appearance of an organism, identifying the gene that has been mutated will provide insight into the normal function of the wild type, or non-mutated, gene. Consider Pfeiffer syndrome, for example. The identification of the gene that, when mutated, leads to the malformations associated with this syndrome will also identify a gene that is likely involved in limb and cranio-facial development. Model organisms are often manipulated experimentally to mutate specific genes so that the effect of these mutations, and therefore the role of the genes, can be examined. Certain model organisms, such as *Drosophila* and zebrafish, have also been subjected to mutagenetic screens. In these types of experiments, the organisms are treated to induce random mutations that often result in organisms with developmental defects. By determining the genes that have been mutated, biologists can then implicate those genes in the normal development of the region of the organism carrying the defect.

other six *HOM* genes are shown in Figure 7.2 on page 80. Interestingly, the *HOM* genes are located very close to one another and are clustered in the fly's genome. Within this cluster of genes, their order along the chromosome reflects the effects of the mutations on the anterior-posterior axis of the fly. Thus, mutations in the left-most (3') genes in the cluster affect the most anterior body parts, and mutations in the right-most (5') genes in the cluster affect more posterior regions of the fly. The expression patterns of these genes during *Drosophila* development is such that they are expressed spatially and temporally in the order in which they sit in their clusters. Genes at the 3' end of the cluster are expressed first and more anteriorly in the developing embryo than the genes at the other end of the cluster (refer again to Figure 7.2).

Vertebrates, including humans, also have versions, or homologues, of the *HOM* genes. In fact, it appears that all animals not only have homologues of these genes, but that the genomic organization and function of these genes is also incredibly well conserved in all animals. The vertebrate genes are called *Hox* genes. Vertebrates, including humans, have considerably more *Hox* genes than are found in *Drosophila*. Rather than having one cluster of eight genes, as does *Drosophila*, humans have four clusters consisting of as many as 13 genes. Also, rather than having names such as *antennapedia* or *ultrabithorax* the vertebrate *Hox* genes are named using a series of letters and numbers. Each of the four clusters has been assigned a letter to identify it. One cluster is known as the *Hoxa* cluster and the others as the *Hoxb*, *Hoxc*, and *Hoxd* clusters. Each gene is also assigned a number to reflect its position relative to the thirteen possible places it can occupy in a particular cluster. For example, the most 3' (or left-most) gene in the *Hoxa* cluster is named *Hoxa1*, the gene at the opposite end of the cluster is named *Hoxa13*.

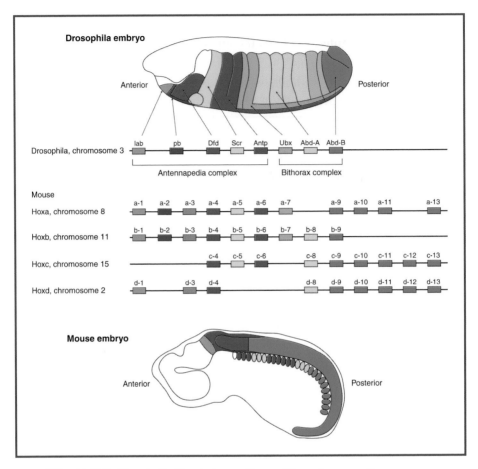

Figure 7.2 The similarities between *Drosophila* and mammalian *Hox* genes in terms of their organization in the genome and expression during development are illustrated here. Homology between genes is represented by color and approximate regions of expression of these genes in the embryos shown is indicated by the same color scheme.

In vertebrates, the expression pattern of the *Hox* genes along the anterior-posterior axis of the developing embryo is consistent with that already described for *Drosophila* and is schematized at the bottom of Figure 7.2 (mouse embryo).

Genes at the 3' end of the cluster are expressed first and more anteriorly (e.g., the hindbrain) than genes more 5' in the cluster which are expressed more caudally. In addition, mutations in the *Hox* clusters are able to produce homeotic phenotypes similar in nature to those observed in *Drosophila*. For example, mice that have had their *Hoxc8* gene mutated exhibit transformations consistent with a homeotic trans-formation. Specifically, the eighth pair of ribs is directly attached to the sternum and an extra fourteenth pair of ribs appears on the first lumbar vertebra, which normally do not have ribs. Both of these transformations are consistent with posterior vertebrae assuming characteristics of more anterior ones. Such homeotic transformations that can be directly attributed to mutations in *Hox* genes have not been described in humans to date. However, the organization, number, and the expression of human *Hox* genes is consistent with their expression in the mouse (Vieille-Grosjean et al., 1997). There is little doubt that these genes are playing the same role in humans as they do in virtually every other animal. In the next chapter, another role of *Hox* genes will be described in terms of limb development, and, in this case, mutations in a human *Hox* gene are described.

The *Hox* genes accomplish this developmental function in anterior-posterior patterning because of the proteins for which they code production: transcription factors. In Chapter 3, the concept of transcription was introduced as the first step in decoding the information in the gene to produce a protein. Transcription factors, such as Hox proteins, essen-tially control when and where other genes are activated or inactivated. Also in Chapter 3, it was mentioned that in general, not all of the 30,000 or so genes that make up the human genome are active in the same cells in the same time. It is because of this differential gene expression that cells can differ in their appearance and function. The factors that control which genes are active and inactive in a given cell, or in a given region of the developing embryo, play an incredibly important role. It is this role of regulator that the products of the *Hox* genes play.

Essentially the *Hox* genes function, then, by being expressed differentially in different regions of the developing embryo. The Hox proteins that these genes code for act as regional control switches that can direct the developmental future of a region of the embryo. They accomplish this by controlling the subsequent genes that will be active in those specific regions. For example, in the *Drosophila antennapedia* mutant, the *Antennapedia* gene, which is normally expressed in the developing abdomen of the fly, becomes active in a region of the head of the developing fly as well. Under normal circumstances, in the developing abdomen, this gene codes for the production of the *antennapedia* protein. This protein then regulates the expression of other genes that confer the identity upon this region of the fly, including the genes required to make legs. When the *antennapedia* protein is produced in the developing head of the fly as a result of a mutation, it performs this same function and regulates the genes required to make legs rather than those genes that would be required to make antennae.

CONNECTIONS

This chapter has examined how the embryonic axes are established and patterned during development. Initially, patterning comes in the form of broadly establishing the anterior-posterior, dorsal-ventral, and left-right axes of the developing embryo. Positional information along the anterior-posterior axis is further refined through the expression and action of the *Hox* genes. This mechanism of action by *Hox* genes and their protein products is conserved, or similar, in virtually all animals, including humans. The *Hox* genes are expressed in specific regions of the embryo, and their protein products are positioned in those same specific regions. The *Hox* proteins are then able to act as molecular switches that regulate the expression of other genes that are, in turn, required to code for the production of all the components of the body associated with that particular region. In *Drosophila*, the action of the *Hom* genes could be in the form of regulating genes that code for the production of legs, wings, or halteres. In vertebrates, the action of the *Hox* genes could result in the regulation of genes that code for the production of specific vertebrae, ribs, or legs.

8

Limb Development

The previous chapters have focused on the events that generate the external and internal layout of the body. This chapter will focus on the development of organs, a process called **organogenesis**. An organ is a part of a body that is formed from two tissues and that carries out a specific function. Examples of organs include the eyes, the heart, and the limbs. The primary focus of this chapter will be on limb development because this area of development is fairly well understood. In addition, the developing limb perfectly illustrates the importance of two different tissues interacting with one another as a developmental mechanism.

THE LIMB BUD

The first morphological indication of limb development is the formation of the limb buds along the trunk of the body. Limb buds form along the trunk of the body where the arms and legs will develop. The majority of the mechanisms used to give rise to a leg or an arm, once their identity has been specified, are similar if not identical. Limb buds first typically appear during the fourth week of human development when specialized cells migrate from the mesoderm adjacent to where the future limbs will be located into what will become the limb bud. These migrating cells originate from two different regions of the mesoderm that make up the trunk of the body.

One of these regions is the mesoderm located on either side of the neural tube and notochord in the trunk of the embryo. This

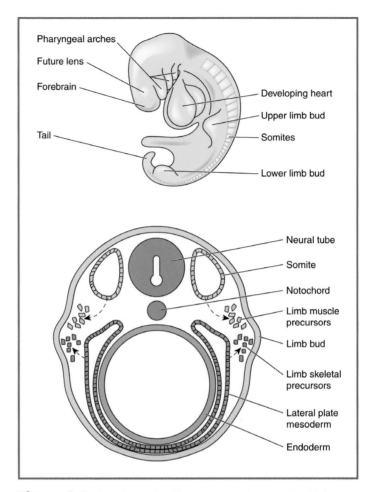

Figure 8.1 A schematic diagram of a four week old human embryo in profile (top) and cross section (bottom) is illustrated here. At this stage, the neural tube is forming, somites are present and the limb buds have appeared. In the cross section, the limb bud can be seen to be populated by mesenchyme that has migrated from the somites as well as lateral plate mesoderm.

mesoderm has a segmental appearance along the anterior-posterior axis, and each of these segments is called a **somite** (Figure 8.1). Mesodermal cells from the somites give rise to the vertebrae and ribs as well as the skeletal muscle of the back, the trunk of the body, and the limbs. The other region of trunk mesoderm that contributes to the developing limb is known as the lateral plate mesoderm. The lateral plate mesoderm lies more ventrally in the trunk, relative to the dorsal somites. The lateral plate mesodermal cells give rise to components of the circulatory system including the heart, blood vessels, and blood, in addition to giving rise to all of the mesodermal components of the limb, other than the musculature.

The specialized cells that are released from the trunk mesoderm to begin limb development are called **mesenchyme**. These cells have the ability to migrate and to actively divide. When limb development is initiated, these mesenchymal cells migrate laterally, eventually accumulating under the ectodermal tissue of the trunk where they form a bud. The limb mesenchymal cells at the distal edge of the limb bud induce a change in the ectoderm that overlies them and that is on the outer surface of the limb bud. This general mechanism of two different tissues, in this case mesoderm and ectoderm, interacting with one another is similar to neural induction where the notochord releases factors to initiate the formation of the neural plate. Similar to the effect that the notochord signals have on the neural plate ectoderm, the signal released by the limb mesenchyme induces the overlying ectodermal cells to elongate as well. The factor that is released by the limb bud mesenchyme is a protein called Fibroblast Growth Factor 10 (FGF10) (Yonei-Tamura et al., 1999).

When FGF10 is released by the mesenchymal cells, it makes its way to the adjacent layer of ectodermal cells where it signals these cells to elongate. The elongated cells form a thickened structure, called the apical ectodermal ridge (AER), which runs along the distal edge of the limb bud. The AER is crucial for limb development because it acts as a signaling center. In much the same way that the mesenchyme of the limb bud induces formation of the AER, the cells of the AER, in turn, produce factors make their way to the adjacent mesenchymal cells where they act as signals or messages that instruct these cells how to act.

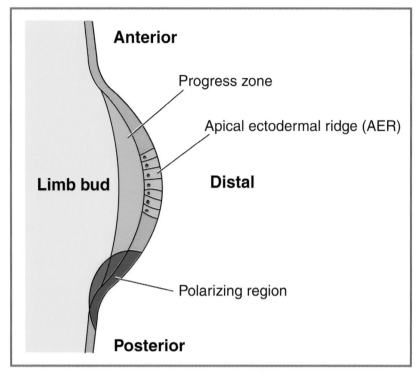

Figure 8.2 Important regions of the developing limb bud include the progress zone, the zone of polarizing activity (polarizing region, or ZPA), and the apical ectodermal ridge (AER). They are illustrated in this diagram.

One of the factors released by the AER is the protein Fibroblast Growth Factor 8 (FGF8). These AER-produced growth factors instruct the adjacent, underlying mesenchyme, a region known as the **progress zone** (Figure 8.2), to continue its growth. The limb grows along a proximal-distal axis where the proximal end of this axis is the trunk of the body and the distal end represents the region of growth which will ultimately culminate with the formation of digits. Experiments performed in chick embryos beautifully illustrate the importance of the AER. The removal of the AER from embryonic chick limbs causes limb development to stop at that particular stage,

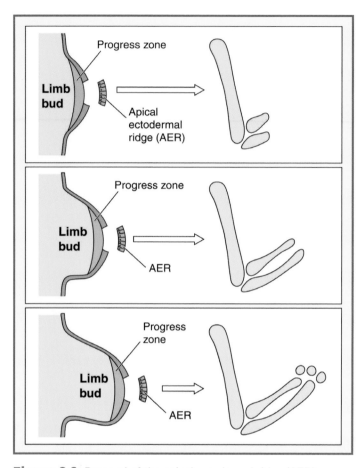

Figure 8.3 Removal of the apical ectodermal ridge (AER) causes limb development to cease at that particular stage and ultimately results in a truncated limb. The degree of truncation depends on how early in development the AER was removed. This diagram shows three examples of three different stages of development.

resulting in a truncated limb (Figure 8.3). The removal of the AER early in development results in a severely truncated limb, and its later removal would result in a more complete limb. In essence, what is occurring in these studies is that the removal of the AER also removes the signal, or signals, for the limb bud to continue its development.

Together, the AER and progress zone lead to the outgrowth along the proximal-distal axis of the developing limb through their communication with each other via released growth factors. Limbs are typically polar structures which means that each end of each axis of the limb is different. Additional mechanisms must exist to pattern this polarity. If one examines the proximal-distal axis of the developing limb, it might be considered that in a very general manner the AER is specifying the distal, or far, end of this axis.

Another one of the axes that must be patterned is the anterior-posterior axis of the limb. The anterior end of this axis corresponds to the future location of the thumb, and the posterior end corresponds to the future location of the pinky finger. This positional information along the anterior-posterior axis initially originates from a region localized at the posterior margin of the limb bud, which is called the **zone of polarizing activity** (ZPA). The cells of the ZPA provide this positional information by producing and releasing a factor that informs cells in the vicinity that they are in the posterior region of the developing limb. The factor produced by the cells of the ZPA is a protein called Sonic Hedgehog (designated Shh). As the importance of the AER can be illustrated in experiments in chick embryos, so can the importance of Shh acting as this polarizing signal that defines that region of the limb bud as being posterior. The addition of the Shh protein to the anterior side of the limb bud, the region opposite that of the ZPA, leads to a mirror image duplication of digits (Figure 8.4) (Riddle et al., 1993). This indicates that Shh is able to induce cells that normally have an anterior identity into cells that have a posterior identity. This essentially disrupts the anterior-posterior axis of the limb bud, such that each end of this axis takes on a posterior identity instead of one end having posterior identity and the other anterior identity.

The mechanism for specifying the remaining dorsal-ventral axis of the limb, where the dorsal region will eventually develop

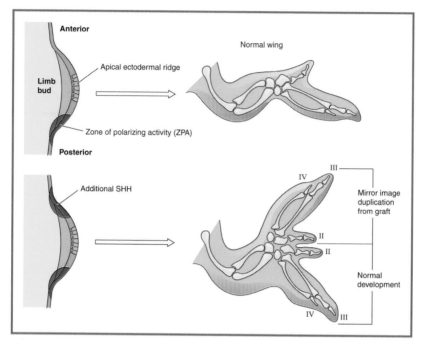

Figure 8.4 The addition of ectopic Sonic Hedgehog (Shh) to the anterior side of the limb bud leads to a mirror image duplication of digits in experiments in chicks (shown in the bottom diagram). The top diagram represents normal development. This finding suggests that Shh can functionally substitute for the zone of polarizing activity.

nails and the ventral region represents the palm or sole, is also similar to what has already been discussed. The dorsal ectoderm of the limb bud produces a protein called Wnt7a. This protein then induces the adjacent dorsal mesenchyme to activate a gene called *Lmx1*. Like the *Hox* genes, *Lmx1* encodes for the production of a transcription factor, and the product of this gene, the Lmx1 protein, is able to regulate additional genes in the dorsal mesenchyme that will act as instructions to produce dorsal structures. In fact, nail-patella syndrome is characterized by a lack of dorsal structures including nails and kneecaps and is found in humans who lack functional *LMX1* (Chen et al., 1998; Dreyer et al., 1998).

The initial establishment of the axes of the limb bud can be seen to be, in part, a result of the interplay between the ectoderm and mesoderm layers that make up that bud. In general, the importance of cells producing factors that can either diffuse to other cells (as in the case of the AER) or that can define regions of the limb bud (as in the case of the ZPA) to induce a response is clear. This general establishment of the axes defines directionality in the limb bud; however, additional factors come in to play to further refine the pattern of the limb. Much like the anterior-posterior axis of the trunk of the embryo is first established and then further refined by the action of the *Hox* genes, so is the developing limb first patterned broadly, by the mechanisms described above, and then refined further by the action of those same *Hox* genes.

If one considers the limbs of a human, a distinct pattern can be observed that is conserved between arms and legs, particularly at the skeletal level (Figure 8.5). Along the proximal-distal axis, both upper arms and legs contain a single bone, the humerus and femur, respectively, that are the most proximal structures. This region of the limb is sometimes referred to as the stylopod. The region of the limb adjacent and distal to this bone, sometimes called the zeugopod, contains the ulna and radius in the forearm and the tibia and fibula in the lower leg. Finally, adjacent and distal to this region is the autopod, which is made up of the wrist, hand, and fingers, or ankle, foot, and toes. The pattern of a human limb from the proximal to distal end is thus made up of at least three distinct segments: the stylopod, zeugopod, and autopod. These limbs develop in a phase-like manner from the proximal to distal direction such that the stylopod develops first followed by the zeugopod and autopod.

During limb development, the *Hox* genes are expressed in the limb bud in a manner consistent with what is observed concerning their expression in the trunk of the body. One major difference is that not all of the *Hox* genes are expressed and only the group 9 to group 13 genes are involved in limb

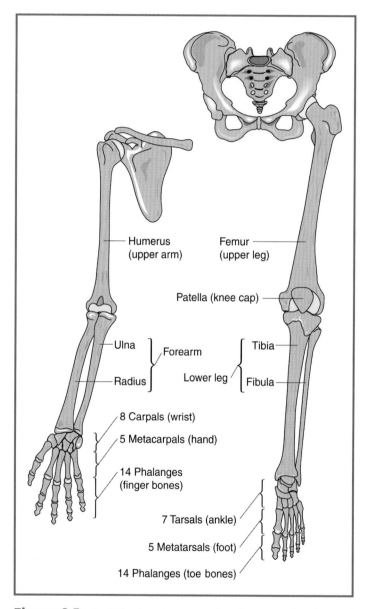

Figure 8.5 A distinct and conserved pattern can be observed between arms and legs, particularly at the skeletal level. For example, the humerus and femur are similar in nature, as are the bones of the forearm and lower leg and the phalanges that make up either the toes or fingers.

patterning. In addition, it seems that only two of the *Hox* clusters are involved rather than all four. The *Hoxd* cluster is typically associated with limb development as is the *Hoxa* cluster to a certain extent. The *Hoxb* and *Hoxc* clusters are not active. Each of the three segments of the developing limb exhibits a particular signature of expression of *Hox* genes. Specific *Hox* genes are expressed during development of the stylopod, a different complement of *Hox* genes is expressed in the developing zeugopod, and still another complement is expressed during autopod development. Just as the disruption of *Hox* gene expression during development of the trunk can have a serious impact on its appearance, so can disruption of *Hox* expression impact the appearance of the limb. For example, mice that do not have the functional *Hoxa-11* and *Hoxd-11* genes completely lack the ulna and radius of their forelimbs.

DIGIT PATTERNING

Interestingly, the *Hox* genes pattern not only the proximal-distal axis of the limb, but also pattern the anterior-posterior axis. The pattern of the limb along the anterior-posterior axis is slightly more obvious, particularly if one examines the order of their fingers and toes. As mentioned previously, the thumb (or big toe) represents the anterior end of the axis and the pinky finger (or little toe) represents the posterior end. As has been observed for the expression along the anterior-posterior axis of the trunk and along the proximal-distal axis of the limb, regions of the developing autopod are also characterized along the anterior-posterior axis by specific signatures of *Hox* gene expression. Transformations in identity of the components of the anterior-posterior axis of the limb have also been characterized in association with disruptions in *Hox* gene function.

Earlier in the book, the physical effects of thalidomide on limb development were discussed. Despite what is known about limb development, however, the exact mechanism by which thalidomide actually acts to disrupt this process is still a

(continued on page 92)

A HUMAN *HOX* MUTATION

Recently, the first human malformation resulting from the disruption of the action of a *Hox* gene was identified. This malformation relates to limb development and is consistent with the homeotic mutations that have been described previously, as would be predicted. Human synpolydactyly syndrome (Figure 8.6) is outwardly characterized by the fusion of digits, the fingers, and toes, in the limb. Recently it was discovered that this syndrome results from mutations in the *HOXD-13* gene (Muragaki et al., 1996). However, the outward appearance of the hands and feet of people who suffer from synpolydactyly syndrome are not necessarily consistent with what might be predicted to be associated with a mutation in a *Hox* gene. Based on what has been observed in other animals, mutations in *Hox* genes could be expected to give rise to homeotic mutations, where one region of the body takes on the identity of another. Closer examination of the hands and feet of people with this syndrome, however, reveals that this syndrome actually is consistent with a homeotic mutation. X-ray analysis of the hands and feet of people suffering from synpolydactyly syndrome reveal the transformation of the bones of the hand into ones that more resemble the bones of the wrist (the metacarpals are transformed into carpals) and the transformation of the bones of the foot into ones that more closely resemble those of the ankle (the metatarsals are transformed into tarsals). These transformations truly are homeotic in nature and represent a region of the limb taking on the identity of another region. This is very much like, in principal, what is seen in other animals with whose *Hox* genes have been mutated: mice carrying a mutation in the *Hoxc8* gene have an extra fourteenth pair of ribs on the first lumbar vertebra which normally do not have ribs or the *bithorax* mutant *Drosophila*, where one segment (or segments) of the fly takes on the identity of another and develops wings rather than halteres.

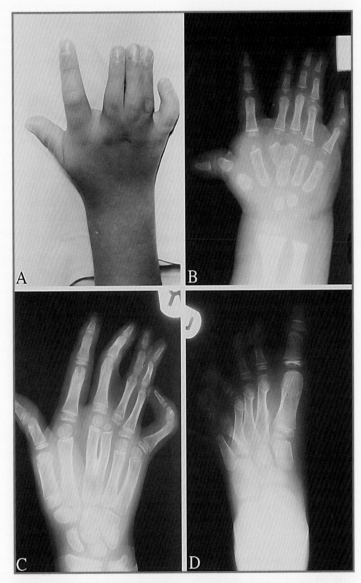

Figure 8.6 A mutation in the human *HOXD13* gene can result in limb malformation. Photographs and X-rays showing hand and foot as a result of this mutation are shown here. Notice the partial fusion of the fingers and toes.

(continued from page 89)
mystery. One hypothesis is that thalidomide inhibits the growth of the limb bud mesenchyme. The inhibition or disruption of the progress zone could potentially lead to phocomelia or the loss of proximal limb structures such as the stylopod and/or zeugopod that characterizes birth defects resulting from exposure to thalidomide. Disruptions in *Hox* patterning along the proximal-distal axis of the limb could also result in this type of malformation. The loss of the ulna and radius, or zeugopod, in the forelimbs of mice that are lacking the functional *Hoxa-11* and *Hoxd-11* genes supports this theory.

CONNECTIONS

The developing limb is a complex process that is dependent on many simultaneously occurring mechanisms. Outgrowth of the limb from the trunk of the body, along the proximal-distal axis, is dependant on the interaction between the AER and progress zone. Because organs are generally formed from two tissues, this interaction between ectoderm (the AER) and mesoderm (the progress zone) is an excellent model that can be used to understand organogenesis. As is observed during patterning of the trunk of the body, early patterning of the limb involves broadly establishing the axes (for example the signals released by the ZPA) and then refining these axes. In fact, this chapter has illustrated how many of the mechanisms that are used during development of the trunk of the body can be used again, in a different context, to control additional aspects of development, in this case, the limbs. For example, the *Hox* genes not only have a role in the specification of where limbs form, they also play a role in the patterning of the anterior-posterior and proximal-dorsal axes of the limb. This is actually a common theme in developmental biology, where mechanisms may be used in different contexts and at different times to accomplish similar functions. Interestingly many of these mechanisms are also well conserved between different animals. In the context of limb development, for example, the genes and their expression and function that have been described here in relation to human development are well conserved between animals as diverse as mice, birds, ourselves, and to a certain extent even fish. It is for this reason that development can provide many insights into what makes organisms similar and what makes them different. Development truly does provide a foundation on which all biology can be built.

Human development begins with the fertilization of an egg by a sperm. During the span of 264 days, this first cell will give rise to many cells that will go on to make important decisions at the molecular and cellular levels as they continue to divide and to take on specific fates. This collection of cells will come to take on form and, as gastrulation occurs, they will begin to position themselves to reflect the eventual role they will take as development proceeds. Axes will form that will define the front and back, left and right, and top and bottom of the developing embryo. The nervous system will form as will organs, and throughout this entire process the embryo and then fetus will continue to grow. This book was able to touch upon only a small number of the many events at the cellular, molecular, and genetic levels that control development. Based on these few highlights, however, there is little doubt that the developmental process by which a single cell becomes an embryo and ultimately an adult organism is delicate and finely balanced. The large number of defects attributed to disruptions of single elements of many of the developmental pathways described in this book clearly indicates how delicate and sensitive the developing embryo is. This delicate nature of development can only add to the awe-inspiring experience that it represents with its limitless number of events and pathways that occur at the cellular, molecular, and genetic levels and that coordinate to produce every multicellular organism.

Glossary

Acrosome A structure at the tip of the sperm head.

Activated Carrier A molecule that contains a particular chemical group, connected by a high energy bond. An activated carrier can donate the energy stored in this bond or of the chemical group itself in many biochemical reactions.

Adenosine triphosphate (ATP) A molecule that is used to store energy for the cell. Is also a building block of DNA.

Amino acid The building blocks of proteins.

Blastocoel The hollow cavity inside the blastocyst.

Blastocyst A hollow ball of cells, making up the pre-embryo, that develops from the morula.

Chorion The outermost layer of cells surrounding the implanted embryo.

Chromosomes Individual threads of DNA found in the nucleus.

Cytoskeleton A network of tubular and filamentous proteins that make up a protein scaffolding that acts as a support for the cell and its shape. It also is used to move the cell and to move molecules within the cell.

Diencephalon The posterior region of the forebrain.

Diploid cell A cell that contains two sets of chromosomes.

DNA (Deoxyribonucleic acid) A nucleic acid made up of building blocks that are in turn made of a ribose sugar and one of the bases: adenine, cytosine, guanine, or thymine. The molecule used as the gentic material by the cell.

Embryo A developing human from the beginning of week three to the end of week eight.

Embryonic disc The band of cells that is positioned between the yolk sac and amniotic cavity that will give rise to the embryo.

Embryonic stage Time from the beginning of week three to the end of week eight.

Endoplasmic reticulum The organelle adjacent to and continuous with the nucleus. It is a network of membranous flattened sacs and tubes and is made up of rough (ribosome-studded) and smooth (ribosome-free) regions.

Epiblast The cells of the inner cell mass that do not contribute to the hypoblast.

Epigenesis The view of development where structures arise progressively.

Fertilization The fusion of sperm and ova that produces the zygote.

Fetus The developing human from the end of the eighth week until birth.

Fibroblast Connective tissue cell.

Gastrulation Developmental process where the cells of the embryo undergo significant movements as they rearrange themselves. These movements ultimately lead to the establishment of the three germ layers.

Gene Regions of DNA that are able to code for the production of protein.

Genome The genetic material of an organism, found in the nucleus.

Germ cell Sperm and ova (eggs).

Golgi apparatus An organelle made up of flattened membranous sacs. It stores, modifies, and packages proteins that have been produced in the endoplasmic reticulum and that will eventually be delivered to some other location within or outside of the cell.

Haploid cell A cell that contains one set of chromosomes.

***Hox* genes** A family of genes found in all animals. These genes are clustered in the genome and are involved antero-posterior patterning.

Hypothalamus The ventral region of the forebrain that coordinates the endocrine and nervous systems.

Inner cell mass Collection of cells found inside the blastocyst.

Mesencephalon The midbrain.

Mesenchyme Connective tissue cells, usually mesoderm, which have the ability to migrate.

Mitochondrion Long oval organelles that are surrounded by an outer membrane and an inner membrane that is folded in upon itself. The "power plants" of the cell.

Mitosis Cell division or cellular reproduction, where one cell divides into two virtually identical daughter cells.

Morphogenesis Processes that alter the shape and form of the embryo.

Morula A solid cluster of cells, making up the pre-embryo, that is produced by cleavage.

Glossary

Neural crest A collection of cells that initially links the newly formed neural tube and overlying ectoderm. Neural crest cells migrate extensively throughout the body during development and also give rise to a large number of cell types and structures.

Neural plate The ectodermal cells that are initially induced by the notochord to become neural ectoderm. In response to this induction, the cells that make up the neural plate take on a distinctly elongated and columnar appearance.

Neurulation The developmental process that gives rise to the neural tube.

Node The knot-like structure at the front of the extending primitive streak.

Notochord A transient rod-like structure of cells that runs along the anterior-posterior axis of the embryo and lies beneath the developing central nervous system.

Nucleus Largest organelle in the cell. It contains the genome.

Oocyte An egg cell.

Optic vesicle Vesicles that develop from the forebrain and that will give rise to the eyes.

Organelle Structures that perform specific functions and that are found in the cytoplasm of eukaryotic cells.

Organogenesis Organ development.

Patterning Ordering cells and structures to produce the pattern of a structure of the body or the body itself. The process used to lay down, or map out, the body plan.

Phocomelia Birth defect characterized by the child's hands and feet being attached to abbreviated, or shortened, arms and legs.

Phospholipid Major kind of lipid used to construct biological membranes.

Placenta The structure that is formed by the chorion, its projections into the endometrium, and the endometrium itself. This structure allows the embryo to obtain nutrients and oxygen from the mother while excreting wastes.

Pluripotent Cell that have the capacity to form any type of human cell or tissue other than those associated with extra-embryonic tissues.

Pre-embryonic stage The first two weeks of human development that precede implantation.

Primitive groove The groove formed when cells move inward and pass through the primitive streak.

Primitive streak A line of cells running along the midline of the embryonic disc during gastrulation.

Progeny Offspring

Progress zone The region of mesenchyme at the distal tip of the developing limb bud.

Prosencephalon The forebrain.

Protein A linear chain of amino acids. Each unique protein is made up of a unique sequence of amino acids.

Rhombencephalon The hindbrain.

Rhombomere A discrete segment that makes up the developing hindbrain.

Ribosome Structure in the cell made of protein and RNA that are involved in translation.

RNA (Ribonucleic acid) A nucleic acid made up of building blocks that are in turn made of a ribose sugar and one of the bases: adenine, cytosine, guanine, or uracil.

Somatic cell Cells, other than germ cells, that make up the body of an organism.

Somite Segmented mesoderm along the anterior-posterior axis of the trunk of the embryo.

Telencephalon The anterior region of the forebrain.

Teratogen Agent that can disrupt development and lead to birth defects.

Thalamus Region of the forebrain that relays sensory information to the cerebrum.

Transcription Copying of the sequence of the coding region of a gene into RNA.

Trophoblast The cell layer that makes up the outer sphere of the blastocyst.

Zona pellucida The protective covering that surrounds the oocyte.

Zone of polarizing activity (ZPA) A region localized at the posterior margin of the limb bud that acts as a signaling center during limb development.

Zygote The fertilized egg.

Bibliography

Alberts, B, et al. *Molecular Biology of the Cell.* New York: Garland Science, 2002.

Campbell, K.H., et al. "Sheep cloned by nuclear transfer from a cultured cell line." *Nature.* 380(6569) (1996): 64-66.

Chen, H., et al. "Limb and kidney defects in Lmx1b mutant mice suggest an involvement of LMX1B in human nail patella syndrome". *Nature Genetics.* 19(1) (1998): 51-55.

Davis, A.P., et al. "Absence of radius and ulna in mice lacking hoxa-11 and hoxd-11." *Nature.* 375(6534) (1995): 791-5.

Dealy, C.N., et al. "Wnt-5a and Wnt-7a are expressed in the developing chick limb bud in a manner suggesting roles in pattern formation along the proximodistal and dorsoventral axes." *Mechanisms of Development.* 43(2-3) (1993): 175-86.

Dreyer, S.D., et al. "Mutations in LMX1B cause abnormal skeletal patterning and renal dysplasia in nail patella syndrome." *Nature Genetics.* 19(1) (1998): 47-50.

Duboule, D. "Making progress with limb models." *Nature.* 418(6897) (2002): 492-493.

Gilbert, S.F. *Developmental Biology.* Sunderland, Mass.: Sinauer Associates, 2000.

Johnson, M.D. *Human Biology Concepts and Current Issues Second Edition.* San Francisco: Benjamin Cummings, 2003.

Kalthoff, K. *Analysis of Biological Development, Second Edition.* New York: McGraw Hill, 2001.

Knightley, P., H. Evans, E. Potter, and M. Wallace. *Suffer the Children: The Story of Thalidomide.* New York: Viking Press. 1979.

Le Mouellic, H., et al. "Homeosis in the mouse induced by a null mutation in the Hox-3.1 gene." *Cell.* 69(2) (1992): 251-264.

Muragaki, Y., et al. "Altered growth and branching patterns in synpolydactyly caused by mutations in HOXD13." *Science.* 272(5261) (1996): 548-551.

Parr, B.A., et al. "Mouse Wnt genes exhibit discrete domains of expression in the early embryonic CNS and limb buds." *Development.* 119(1) (1993): 247-261.

Prentice, D.A. *Stem Cells and Cloning.* San Francisco: Benjamin Cummings, 2003.

Riddle, R.D., et al. "Sonic hedgehog mediates the polarizing activity of the ZPA." *Cell.* 75(7) (1993): 1401-1416.

Riddle, R.D. and C. Tabin. "How limbs develop." *Scientific American.* 280(2) (1999): 74-79.

Saunders, J.W.J. "The proximo-distal sequence of origin of the parts of the chick wing and the role of the ectoderm." *Journal of Experimental Zoology.* 108 (1948): 363-403.

Stephens, T.D. *Dark Remedy: The Impact of Thalidomide and its Revival as a Vital Medicine.* Cambridge, Mass.: Perseus Publishers, 2001.

Sulik, K., et al. "Morphogenesis of the murine node and notochordal plate." *Developmental Dynamics.* 201(3) (1994): 260-278.

Thorogood, P. *Embryos, Genes, and Birth Defects.* Chichester, N.Y.: J. Wiley, 1997.

Ulijaszek, S.J., et al. *The Cambridge Encyclopedia of Human Growth and Development.* Cambridge, U.K.; New York, N.Y.: Cambridge University Press, 1998.

Vieille-Grosjean, I., et al. "Branchial HOX gene expression and human craniofacial development." *Dev Biol.* 183(1) (1997): 49-60.

Wolpert, L. *The Triumph of the Embryo.* Oxford; New York: Oxford University Press, 1991.

Wolpert, L. *Principles of Development. 2nd ed.* Oxford: Oxford University Press, 2002.

Yonei-Tamura, S., et al. "FGF7 and FGF10 directly induce the apical ectodermal ridge in chick embryos." *Developmental Biology.* 211(1) (1999): 133-143.

Further Reading

Nature Special Issue. "The Human Genome." 15 February 2001. Vol. 409. 745–964.

Science Special Issue. "Stem Cell Research and Ethics." 25 February 2000. Vol. 287 (#5457). 1353-1544.

Science Special Issue. "The Human Genome." 16 February 2001. Vol. 291 (#5507). 1145-1434.

Nova Special: "Life's Greatest Miracle." Originally broadcast November 20, 2001 (also see http://www.pbs.org/wgbh/nova/miracle/).

Websites

Medline Plus, part of the U.S. National Institutes of Health and the National Library of Medicine. Information on Birth Defects. *http://www.nlm.nih.gov/medlineplus/birthdefects.html*

Illinois Teratogen Information Service, information on teratogens and human development.
http://www.fetal-exposure.org/

Virtual Library of Developmental Biology, by Scott Gilbert (author of *Developmental Biology*).
http://zygote.swarthmore.edu/

Website details the stages of fetal development.
http://www.w-cpc.org/fetal.html

Society for Developmental Biology
http://sdb.bio.purdue.edu/index.html

The Virtual Embryo. Interactive information about developmental biology
http://www.ucalgary.ca/UofC/eduweb/virtualembryo/

Unit (metric)		Metric to English	English to Metric	
LENGTH				
Kilometer	km	1 km 0.62 mile (mi)	1 mile (mi)	1.609 km
Meter	m	1 m 3.28 feet (ft)	1 foot (ft)	0.305 m
Centimeter	cm	1 cm 0.394 inches (in)	1 inch (in)	2.54 cm
Millimeter	mm	1 mm 0.039 inches (in)	1 inch (in)	25.4 mm
Micrometer	μm			
WEIGHT (MASS)				
Kilogram	kg	1 kg 2.2 pounds (lbs)	1 pound (lbs)	0.454 kg
Gram	g	1 g 0.035 ounces (oz)	1 ounce (oz)	28.35 g
Milligram	mg			
Microgram	μg			
VOLUME				
Liter	L	1 L 1.06 quarts	1 gallon (gal)	3.785 L
			1 quart (qt)	0.94 L
			1 pint (pt)	0.47 L
Milliliter	mL or cc	1 mL 0.034 fluid ounce (fl oz)	1 fluid ounce (fl oz)	29.57 mL
Microliter	μL			
TEMPERATURE				
$°C = 5/9 (°F - 32)$		$°F = 9/5 (°C + 32)$		

Index

Index

Index

Picture Credits

About the Author

Dr. Ted Zerucha was educated at the University of Manitoba in Winnipeg, Canada, and at the University of Ottawa in Ottawa, Canada. He received his Bachelor of Science Honors degree from the Department of Biochemistry and Masters of Science degree from the Department of Microbiology, both at the University of Manitoba. He earned his Ph.D. in 1999 from the Department of Cellular and Molecular Medicine/ Anatomy and Neurobiology at the University of Ottawa, where he studied at the Loeb Health Research Institute of the Ottawa Hospital. Following research positions at the University of Chicago and at Argonne National Laboratory, he joined the Biology Department of Keene State College, where he teaches courses based on his primary research interests, developmental and evolutionary biology and cellular and molecular biology. Dr. Zerucha has published a number of research papers, including articles in the *Journal of Neuroscience, Mechanisms of Development, Biochemistry and Cell Biology,* and *Nucleic Acids Research.* He has also had his work presented at a large number of conferences across North America and Europe.